Check you know it all with CGP!

Quick question — do you own CGP's
Knowledge Organiser for AQA GCSE Spanish?

You do? ¡Estupendo! Now you can use this Knowledge Retriever
to check you've got everything stuck in your brain.

There are memory tests for each topic, plus mixed quiz questions
to make extra sure you've really remembered all the crucial points. Enjoy.

CGP — still the best! ☺

Our sole aim here at CGP is to produce the highest quality books —
carefully written, immaculately presented and dangerously close to being funny.

Then we work our socks off to get them out to you
— at the cheapest possible prices.

Contents

Published by CGP.

Editors: Siân Butler, Gabrielle Richardson, Hannah Roscoe, Matt Topping.
Contributor: Jacqui Richards.

With thanks to Becca Lakin for the proofreading.
With thanks to Lottie Edwards for the copyright research.

ISBN: 978 1 78908 720 8

Printed by Elanders Ltd, Newcastle upon Tyne.
Clipart from Corel®

Based on the classic CGP style created by Richard Parsons

How to Use This Book

Every page in this book has a matching page in the GCSE Spanish **Knowledge Organiser**.
Before using this book, try to **memorise** everything on a Knowledge Organiser page.
Then follow these **seven steps** to see how much knowledge you're able to retrieve...

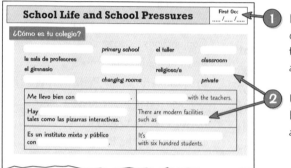

1 In this book, there are two versions of each page. Find the **'First Go'** of the page you've tried to memorise, and write the **date** at the top.

2 Use what you've learned from the Knowledge Organiser to **fill in** any dotted lines or white spaces.

3 Use the Knowledge Organiser to **check your work**.
Use a **different coloured pen** to write in anything you missed or that wasn't quite right. This lets you see clearly what you **know** and what you **don't know**.

4 After doing the 'First Go' page, **wait a few days**. This is important because **spacing out** your retrieval practice helps you to remember things better.

5 Now do the **'Second Go'** page.
The 'Second Go' page is harder — it has more things missing.

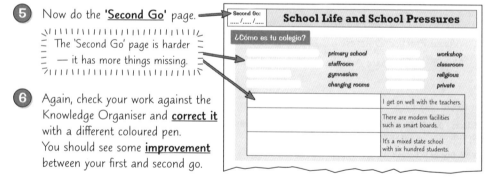

6 Again, check your work against the Knowledge Organiser and **correct it** with a different coloured pen.
You should see some **improvement** between your first and second go.

7 **Wait** another few days, then try recreating the whole Knowledge Organiser page on a **blank piece of paper**. If you can do this, you'll know you've **really learned it**.

There are also **Mixed Practice Quizzes** dotted throughout the book:
• The quizzes come in sets of four. They test a mix of content from the previous few pages.
• Do each quiz on a different day — write the date you do each one at the top of the quiz.
• Tick the questions you get right and record your score in the box at the end.

Numbers

Los números

TICKET #	TICKET #	TICKET #	TICKET #
14		**73**	
	veintinueve		ciento treinta

TICKET #	TICKET #	TICKET #	TICKET #
	1942		**3816**
cuatrocientos cincuenta		dos mil diez	

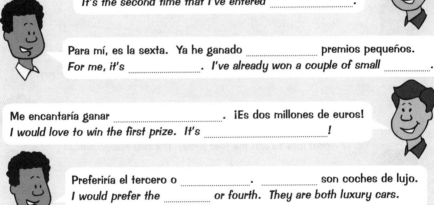

Es .... que he jugado a la lotería.
It's the second time that I've entered ....

Para mí, es la sexta. Ya he ganado .... premios pequeños.
For me, it's .... I've already won a couple of small ....

Me encantaría ganar .... ¡Es dos millones de euros!
I would love to win the first prize. It's .... !

Preferiría el tercero o .... son coches de lujo.
I would prefer the .... or fourth. They are both luxury cars.

Number phrases

una docena			*to add*
	some / a few / about	el/la máximo/a	
numeroso/a		el/la mínimo/a	
	several		*percent*
ambos/as		una cifra	

 ☑ ☑ ☑

4

Numbers

Los números

TICKET #	TICKET #	TICKET #	TICKET #
14	**29**	**73**	**130**

TICKET #	TICKET #	TICKET #	TICKET #
450	**1942**	**2010**	**3816**

It's the second time that I've entered the lottery.

For me, it's the sixth. I've already won a couple of small prizes.

I would love to win the first prize. It's two million euros!

I would prefer the third or fourth. They are both luxury cars.

Number phrases

a dozen

some / a few / about

numerous

several

both

to add

maximum

minimum

percent

figure (e.g. 1)

 ✓ ✓   ✓

Times and Dates

¿Qué hora es?

.... El partido termina a las siete menos cuarto.
It's quarter past six. The match finishes ....

Empieza a la una así que debemos partir ....
It starts .... *so we must set off at half past eleven.*

Many Spanish-speaking countries also use the 24-hour clock.

.... treinta minutos.   *It's 21:30.*

Son las tres horas catorce minutos.   *It's* ....

Son las diecinueve horas ....   *It's 19:55.*

Useful time phrases

Tengo un examen	I have an exam the day after tomorrow.
Está en oferta durante quince días.	It's on offer for ....
Voy al gimnasio	I go to the gym every three days.
Anoche, fui al teatro en el centro.	.... , I went to the theatre in the town centre.
.... , voy de compras con mi hermanastro.	This afternoon, I'm going shopping with my stepbrother.
El año pasado, viajé a Polonia para .... mis abuelos.	.... , I travelled to Poland to visit my grandparents.
Nos conocimos	We met the day before yesterday.
.... ir al mercado mañana por la mañana.	We have to go to the market ....

 ☑   ☑ ☺ ☑

Times and Dates

¿Qué hora es?

It's quarter past six. The match finishes at quarter to seven.

It starts at one o'clock so we must set off at half past eleven.

Many Spanish-speaking countries also use

It's 21:30.

It's 03:14.

It's 19:55.

Useful time phrases

	I have an exam the day after tomorrow.
	It's on offer for a fortnight.
	I go to the gym every three days.
	Last night, I went to the theatre in the town centre.
	This afternoon, I'm going shopping with my stepbrother.
	Last year, I travelled to Poland to visit my grandparents.
	We met the day before yesterday.
	We have to go to the market tomorrow morning.

Times and Dates

Los días de la semana

_____	Monday
martes	_____
_____	Wednesday
	Thursday
viernes	_____
_____	Saturday
domingo	_____

_____,'
cogimos el tren a Buñol.
At the weekend,
we took the train to Buñol.

Los miércoles, voy al
cine con mis amigos.
_____, I go
to the cinema with my friends.

Los meses del año

enero	_____	_____	May	_____	September
	February	junio	_____	octubre	_____
marzo	_____	julio	_____	_____	November
	April		_____	August	diciembre	_____

En invierno, iremos a esquiar.	_____, we will go skiing.
_____ es mi estación preferida.	Spring is my favourite _____.
Cada verano, me gusta montar a caballo.	_____, I like to go horse riding.
A mis padres y a mí nos encanta ir de pesca _____.	My parents and I love to go fishing in autumn.

¿Qué fecha es?

In Spanish, you say 'the three of May' not 'the third of May'. This applies
to all dates apart from '_____', which uses 'el primero de' or '_____'.

_____
(on) the third of May

Es el primero de / _____ febrero.
It's _____.

Times and Dates

Los días de la semana

_____	Monday
_____	Tuesday
_____	Wednesday
_____	Thursday
_____	Friday
_____	Saturday
_____	Sunday

At the weekend,
we took the train to Buñol.

On Wednesdays, I go to
the cinema with my friends.

Los meses del año

_____ January	_____ May	_____ September
_____ February	_____ June	_____ October
_____ March	_____ July	_____ November
_____ April	_____ August	_____ December

	In winter, we will go skiing.
	Spring is my favourite season.
	Every summer, I like to go horse riding.
	My parents and I love to go fishing in autumn.

¿Qué fecha es?

In Spanish, you say '_____' not 'the third of May'. This applies
to all dates apart from 'the first', which uses '_____' or '_____'.

(on) the third of May	It's the first of February.

 ✓ ✓ ✓

Questions

Asking questions

Put question marks at the beginning and end of a statement to make it a question.

¿Tu corbata es azul?   .... *your tie blue?*   ⟵ Raise your voice
to show it's a question.

Remember that question words need accents.

¿ .... se dice 'cake' en español?   *How do you say 'cake' in Spanish?*

¿Cuándo es tu cumpleaños?   .... *is your birthday?*

¿ .... haces eso?   *Why are you doing that?*

¿Cuántos/as tienes?   .... *do you have?*

¿De .... eres?   *Where are you from?*

¿Quién va?   .... *is going?*

¿ .... es?   *How much is it?*   ⟵ If 'cuánto' is followed by a
..............., it needs to agree, e.g.
¿ .... agua bebes al día?

Tengo una pregunta

¿ .... hoy?	What day is it today?
¿Cuántos años tiene tu primo?	.... your cousin?
¿ .... empieza?	At what time does it start?
¿Por cuánto tiempo has estado aquí?	.... have you been here?
¿ .... tu fruta favorita?	What is your favourite fruit?
¿De qué color era el abrigo?	.... was the coat?
¿ .... este cuadro de Picasso?	How much is this painting by Picasso worth?

Topic 1 — General Stuff

Questions

Asking questions

Put ☐ at the beginning and end of a statement to make it a question.

Is your tie blue? ← ☐ at the end to show it's a question.

Remember that question words need ☐ .

How do you say 'cake' in Spanish?

When is your birthday?

Why are you doing that?

How many do you have?

Where are you from?

Who is going?

How much is it? ← If '☐' is followed by a noun, ☐ , e.g. ¿Cuánta agua bebes al día?

Tengo una pregunta

	What day is it today?
	How old is your cousin?
	At what time does it start?
	How long have you been here?
	What is your favourite fruit?
	What colour was the coat?
	How much is this painting by Picasso worth?

Being Polite

Los saludos

☐	good day / good morning
☐	good afternoon / good evening
buenas noches	☐

hasta luego ☐   see you on Monday

☐   see you tomorrow

hasta pronto

¿...........? / ¿...........?   ¿Cómo está?
How are you? (informal)   ....? (formal)

(no) muy bien
(not) ....

.... so-so

fatal
....

Por favor y gracias

muchas gracias ☐   por favor ☐

☐   That's very kind of you. (informal)   ☐ You're welcome.

Lo siento mucho.   I'm really ....

That's very kind of you. (formal)   ☐   OK

¡Claro!   ☐

¡Por favor! / ¡Perdone!
...........! (E.g. for
asking someone ....)

¡...........!
Excuse me! (E.g. for wanting
to get past someone)

Le presento a...

Le presento a Ana.
.... Ana?   ⟵ Use '<u>Te</u> presento a...' with someone you call ' ☐ '.

.... Arturo.
This is Arturo.   ⟵ Use 'Est<u>a</u> es...' for introducing someone ☐ .

Encantado.
....   ⟵ Use 'Encantad<u>a</u>' if you're ☐ .
You can also say 'mucho gusto', which ☐ for both genders.

Being Polite

Los saludos

good day /
good morning

good afternoon /
good evening

good night

see you later

see you on Monday

see you tomorrow

see you soon

How are you? (informal)   How are you? (formal)

     (not) very well   so-so   terrible

Por favor y gracias

thank you very much

That's very kind of
you. (informal)

That's very kind of
you. (formal)

please

You're welcome.

I'm really sorry.

OK

Of course!

Excuse me! (E.g. for
asking someone the way)

Excuse me! (E.g. for wanting
to get past someone)

Le presento a...

May I introduce Ana?

This is Arturo.

Pleased to meet you.

← Use '   '
with someone you call 'tú'.

← Use '   ' for
introducing someone female.

← Use '   ' if you're female.
You can also say '   ',
which stays the same for both genders.

Being Polite

Asking for things politely

Use ' .... ' ('I would like')
to ask for something politely.

.... un café.
I would like a coffee.

Quisiera hablar.
....

You can also use the verb
'poder' (' .... ').

¿Puedo sentarme?
....?

¿ .... al baño?
May I go to the toilet?

Tú y usted

There are four different ways to say 'you' in Spanish.

1 ' .... ' — for one person who's your .... ,
a family member or of a similar age.

¿Dónde ....?
Where are you?

¿Qué opinas?
What ....?

2 ' .... ' — for a group of two or more people that you know.
Only use ' .... ' if the whole group is female.

¿Dónde estáis?
Where ....?

¿Qué ....?
What do you think?

3 ' .... ' — for one person who's older than you or someone you
don't know. It uses the ' .... ' part of the verb.

¿Dónde ....?
Where are you?

¿Qué opina?
What ....?

4 ' .... ' — for a group of two or more people that you don't know.
It uses the ' .... ' part of the verb.

¿Dónde están?
Where ....?

¿Qué ....?
What do you think?

Being Polite

Asking for things politely

Use '_____' ('I would like')
to ask for something _____ .

> I would like a coffee.

> I would like to talk.

You can also use the verb
'_____' ('to be able to').

> May I sit down?

> May I go to the toilet?

Tú y usted

There are four different ways to say 'you' in Spanish.

1 '_____' — for one person who's _____ ,
a family member or of _____ .

> Where are you?

> What do you think?

2 '_____' — for _____ of two or more people that _____ .
Only use '_____' if the whole group is female.

> Where are you?

> What do you think?

3 '_____' — for one person who's _____ or someone you
don't know. It uses the '_____' part of the verb.

> Where are you?

> What do you think?

4 '_____' — for _____ of two or more people that you don't know.
It uses the '_____' part of the verb.

> Where are you?

> What do you think?

Topic 1 — General Stuff

  ✓ ✓ 😄 ✓

Opinions

¿Qué piensas de..?

¿.............................. mi bolso?
What do you think of my bag?

¿Lo encuentras entretenido?
.... **entertaining?**

¿Cuál es tu opinión de esta canción? .... **of this song?**

El deporte . sea emocionante.	Sport bores me. I don't think it's .
Me parece y .	fun and it makes me laugh.
Es verdad. Las telenovelas .	. I don't like soap operas at all.
No estoy de acuerdo. esta novela es genial.	. I think this novel is .
Me encantan las películas de aventura porque son .	adventure films because they're wonderful.
los documentales.	Documentaries interest me.
Encuentro el pescado .	fish unpleasant.
la fruta. Prefiero las verduras.	I hate fruit. vegetables.

Creo que es...

fantastic   precioso/a

fenomenal   increíble

cool   interesting

perfect   horrible

impresionante   boring

nice, kind   raro/a

fabuloso/a   ridículo/a

pretty   disappointing

Opinions

¿Qué piensas de..?

What do you think of my bag?

Do you find it entertaining?

What is your opinion of this song?

	Sport bores me. I don't think it's exciting.
	I think it's fun and it makes me laugh.
	It's true. I don't like soap operas at all.
	I don't agree. I think this novel is brilliant.
	I love adventure films because they're wonderful.
	Documentaries interest me.
	I find fish unpleasant.
	I hate fruit. I prefer vegetables.

Creo que es...

	fantastic		beautiful
	great		incredible
	cool		interesting
	perfect		awful
	impressive		boring
	nice, kind		strange
	fabulous		ridiculous
	pretty		disappointing

Mixed Practice Quizzes

Personally, I found this section brilliantly useful. Try these quizzes to see what you can remember from p.3-16, then add up your scores to see how you did.

Quiz 1   Date: ...... / ...... / ......

1) 'We like adventure films because they're exciting.'
   How would you say this in Spanish?

2) True or false? 'Los jueves' means 'on Thursday'.

3) Your friend asks you what time it is. Tell them it's 17:30 in Spanish.

4) What does 'Te presento a Naiara' mean in English?

5) Give the English for: 'ochenta y tres por ciento'.

6) How would you ask how much something costs in Spanish?

7) True or false? The formal plural 'you' in Spanish is 'ustedes'.

8) Translate into Spanish: 'Autumn is her favourite season.'

9) You want to get past someone in the street. What do you say in Spanish?

10) 'Vamos al teatro pasado mañana.' What does this mean in English?

Total:

Quiz 2   Date: ...... / ...... / ......

1) How would you politely say that you'd like a coffee in Spanish?

2) '¿A qué hora salís esta noche?' What does this mean in English?

3) Give the Spanish for: 'I won the second prize. It was ninety-five euros.'

4) Say this in Spanish: 'She doesn't like that novel because it's ridiculous.'

5) Translate into English: 'La tienda se cierra a las siete menos diez.'

6) In Spanish, how would you say 'See you soon'?

7) 'Compré una docena de huevos y un par de piñas.' What does this mean?

8) True or false? 'Decepcionante' means 'deceptive' in English.

9) In Spanish, how would you ask a group of two or more
   people that you know what they think about your coat?

10) Your stepdad says: 'Hoy es el once de julio.' What is he saying?

Total:

Mixed Practice Quizzes

Quiz 3   Date: ...... / ...... / ......

1) 'Anoche, Hermine decidió ir al cine. Anteayer, fue a la playa.'
   What did Hermine do first? Explain how you know.

2) '¿Por cuánto tiempo ha sido casado?' What does this mean?

3) How would you say that you went fishing at the weekend in Spanish?

4) In English, what year is 'mil novecientos cincuenta y cuatro'?

5) Give the Spanish for: 'We think soap operas are very entertaining.'

6) Translate into Spanish: 'They both have an exam tomorrow morning.'

7) Your friend tells you 'eres muy amable'. What does this mean?

8) In Spanish, ask politely if you can go to the toilet.

9) Translate into English: '¿Cómo vas a celebrar tu cumpleaños?'

10) Give two informal ways of asking someone how they are in Spanish.

Total:

Quiz 4   Date: ...... / ...... / ......

1) 'This is the third time that Jaime has won the lottery.' Say this in Spanish.

2) Give the two meanings of 'buenos días' in English.

3) What do each of these adjectives mean in English?
   a) fenomenal   b) precioso   c) agradable   d) raro

4) If 'Soy de Portugal' is the answer, what is the question?

5) Which form of the verb does 'usted' use?

6) Translate into English: 'El domingo, voy a montar a caballo.'

7) Translate into Spanish: 'You (form. pl.) hate vegetables and fish.'

8) 'Mi cumpleaños es en febrero.' What does this mean in English?

9) Give the Spanish for: 'What colour is your hat?'

10) 'Last year, I met my stepbrother and his family.' Say this in Spanish.

Total:

About Yourself and Your Family

Preséntate

Mi nombre es Gustavo. Mi _____ es Jiménez. Tengo
quince años y mi _____ es _____ .
My _____ is Gustavo. My surname is Jiménez.
_____ and my birthday is 6th May.

¡Hola! Me llamo Samira. Mi _____
es el 19 de junio de 2006. Cumpliré quince años la
semana que viene, así que somos _____ .
Hello! _____ Samira. My date of birth is 19th June
2006. _____ 15 next week, so we're the same age.

Nací en México, pero ahora soy de _____ española.
_____ in Mexico but now I'm of Spanish nationality.

Soy de Vigo. Mis padres _____ Marruecos antes de que yo naciera.
_____ Vigo. My parents moved from Morocco before I was born.

Háblame de tu familia

	father		stepbrother
la madre			stepsister
	parents	el/la hijo/a único/a	
	brother		twin
la hermana		el marido / el esposo	
	stepfather	/ la esposa	wife
la madrastra		el sobrino	

Tengo muchos [ ].	I have lots of relatives.
Mis abuelos tienen seis [ ] y veintiún [ ].	My [ ] have six children and twenty-one grandchildren.
En total, tengo ocho tíos, diez [ ] y veinte [ ].	In total, I have eight [ ], ten aunts and twenty younger cousins.
También tengo una sobrina joven.	I also have [ ].

About Yourself and Your Family

Preséntate

My name is Gustavo. My surname is Jiménez.
I'm 15 years old and my birthday is 6th May.

Hello! I'm called Samira. My date of birth is 19th June 2006. I'll turn 15 next week, so we're the same age.

I was born in Mexico but now I'm of Spanish nationality.

I'm from Vigo. My parents moved from Morocco before I was born.

Háblame de tu familia

father		stepbrother	
mother		stepsister	
parents		only child	
brother		twin	
sister		husband	
stepfather		wife	
stepmother		nephew	

	I have lots of relatives.
	My grandparents have six children and twenty-one grandchildren.
	In total, I have eight uncles, ten aunts and twenty younger cousins.
	I also have a young niece.

Describing People

El aspecto físico

Mi abuelo es _____ y bastante gordo. Es viejo y _____.
My grandfather is bald and quite _____. He's _____ and wears glasses.

Mi madre tiene el pelo moreno y rizado.
My mother has _____.

Mi prima es _____.
Tiene los ojos marrones y _____.
Lleva maquillaje.
My cousin is really tall.
She has _____ and long, black hair.

Soy de altura mediana. Soy _____ y _____. Soy ciego de un ojo.
I am _____. I'm slim and I don't have freckles. I'm _____ in one eye.

Mi hermano tiene el pelo _____. Es guapo y no tiene barba.
My brother has chestnut-brown hair. He's _____ and he doesn't have a _____.

Mi padre tiene el pelo _____ y un bigote. Es sordo del oído izquierdo.
My father has short hair and a _____. He is _____ in his left ear.

Mi primo es _____. Es bajo y tiene los ojos verdes.
My cousin is red-haired. He's _____ and he has _____.

Mi hermana tiene el pelo liso y _____ y _____.
Utiliza una silla de ruedas.
My sister has _____, blonde hair and blue eyes.
She uses a _____.

22

Describing People

El aspecto físico

My grandfather is bald and quite fat. He's old and wears glasses.

My mother has dark, curly hair.

I am medium height. I'm slim and I don't have freckles. I'm blind in one eye.

My cousin is really tall. She has brown eyes and long, black hair. She wears make-up.

My brother has chestnut-brown hair. He's good-looking and he doesn't have a beard.

My father has short hair and a moustache. He is deaf in his left ear.

My cousin is red-haired. He's short and he has green eyes.

My sister has straight, blonde hair and blue eyes. She uses a wheelchair.

Personalities

Mi personalidad

animado/a

[____]

[____]

happy

affectionate

comprensivo/a

[____]

polite

gracioso/a

[____]

[____]

chatty / talkative

daring / cheeky

serio/a

[____]

sensible

[____]

valiente

egoísta

[____]

perezoso/a

[____]

torpe

[____]

[____]

quiet

[____]

[____]

rude

[____]

naughty

[____]

jealous

Describir personas

Mis padres son .... y .... Mi madre
es habladora pero mi padre es más callado y ....
*My parents are understanding and kind. My mother
is .... but my father is .... and more serious.*

Mi hermana es muy atrevida y
mi hermano es ....
*My sister is .... and
my brother is quite clumsy.*

→

Me gustaría ser más ....
y aventurero como mi hermana.
.... *braver and more*
.... *like my sister.*

Mis profesoras son simpáticas pero .... al mismo tiempo.
My teachers are .... but strict ....

Mi mejor amiga es siempre alegre.	My best friend is always [____] .
Tiene un [____] y es sensible.	She has a good sense of humour and she's [____] .
Sin embargo, a veces es un poco maleducada...	[____] , sometimes she's [____] ...
...porque [____] cuando vamos al cine.	...because she arrives late when we go to the cinema.
Lo encuentro muy frustrante.	I find it very [____] .

Personalities

Mi personalidad

lively	sensitive
happy	quiet
affectionate	brave
understanding	selfish
polite	rude
funny	lazy
chatty / talkative	naughty
daring / cheeky	clumsy
serious	jealous

Describir personas

My parents are understanding and kind. My mother is chatty but my father is quieter and more serious.

My sister is very daring and my brother is quite clumsy. ⟶ I'd like to be braver and more adventurous like my sister.

My teachers are nice but strict at the same time.

	My best friend is always happy.
	She has a good sense of humour and she's sensitive.
	However, sometimes she's a bit rude...
	...because she arrives late when we go to the cinema.
	I find it very frustrating.

 ✓ ✓ ✓

Relationships and Partnership

Las relaciones

_____ con mis padres... ...debido a la barrera generacional.	I don't get on well with my parents... ...due to the _____.
No aguanto a mi hermano y _____ mucho.	_____ my brother and we fight a lot.
Mi hermana _____.	My sister annoys me.
A menudo me relaciono con mi tía.	_____ with my aunt.
Conozco muy bien a mi novia... ...y _____.	_____ my girlfriend really well... ...and I trust her.
Fue amor a primera vista... ...y tenemos _____.	It was _____... ...and we have few arguments.

En el futuro...

Estoy contenta de _____ y el estado civil no me importa demasiado.
_I am happy being single and _____ doesn't matter too much to me._

A mi modo de ver, no es necesario _____ antes de
_____, pero me gustaría hacerlo de todos modos.
_____, it's not necessary to get married
_before having children, but I'd like to do it _____._

Quiero comprometerme porque _____ de mi novio.
Desde mi punto de vista, las bodas son muy _____.
_I want _____ because I'm in love with my boyfriend._
_From my point of view, _____ are very romantic._

Debo admitir que _____ y
los anillos me parecen demasiado caros.
_I must admit that weddings and _____
seem far too expensive to me.

En mi opinión, el matrimonio
te da estabilidad.
_In my opinion, _____
_gives you _____._

_____ suficiente dinero, preferiría comprar una casa con mi _____.
_When I have enough money, I'd prefer _____ with my partner._

Relationships and Partnership

Las relaciones

	I don't get on well with my parents... ...due to the generation gap.
	I can't stand my brother and we fight a lot.
	My sister annoys me.
	I am often in contact with my aunt.
	I know my girlfriend really well... ...and I trust her.
	It was love at first sight... ...and we have few arguments.

En el futuro...

I am happy being single and marital status doesn't matter too much to me.

The way I see it, it's not necessary to get married before having children, but I'd like to do it anyway.

I want to get engaged because I'm in love with my boyfriend. From my point of view, weddings are very romantic.

I must admit that weddings and rings seem far too expensive to me.

In my opinion, marriage gives you stability.

When I have enough money, I'd prefer to buy a house with my partner.

Topic 2 — Me, My Family and Friends

Mixed Practice Quizzes

It's time to form a brave new partnership with some more quizzes — I'm sure it'll be love at first sight. Test yourself on p.19-26 and note down your scores.

Quiz 1   Date: ...... / ...... / ......

1) How do you say 'My uncle has freckles and a beard' in Spanish?
2) Translate into English: 'Tengo veintidós años.'
3) Give the Spanish for 'to be in love with'.
4) What does 'Mi sobrino es perezoso' mean in English?
5) True or false? In Spanish, 'straight, brown hair' is 'el pelo liso y negro'.
6) Give the English for: 'Mi nombre es Nicola. Soy baja y llevo gafas.'
7) In Spanish, give three positive personality traits.
8) Give the Spanish for: 'I would like to be less clumsy.'
9) How do you say 'I get on well with my grandparents' in Spanish?
10) Translate into English: 'Tengo dos hermanos menores.'

Total:

Quiz 2   Date: ...... / ...... / ......

1) 'Mi gemela tiene dos hijas.' How do you say this in English?
2) Give three different eye colours in Spanish.
3) What is the Spanish for 'I would prefer to get married'?
4) Give the English for: 'Me gustaría ser más comprensivo.'
5) What is the Spanish for 'I was born in Lincoln'?
6) How do you say 'Sometimes my best friend annoys me' in Spanish?
7) 'Mi madrastra nunca lleva maquillaje.' Say this in English.
8) Give your date of birth in Spanish.
9) Translate into English: 'Confío en mi novio.'
10) If the adjective 'alegre' was used to describe two women, what ending would it have?

Total:

Mixed Practice Quizzes

Quiz 3 | Date: ...... / ...... / ......

1) 'I have a mother and a stepfather.' Say this in Spanish. ☐
2) Translate into English: 'El marido de mi hermana es bajo.' ☐
3) How would you ask someone what they are called in Spanish? ☐
4) Answer this question in Spanish: '¿Cuántos primos tienes?' ☐
5) Translate into English: 'Me gustaría casarme delante de mi familia y mis amigos porque sería muy romántico.' ☐
6) Give the Spanish for: 'Sometimes I use a wheelchair.' ☐
7) Describe your personality in two Spanish sentences. ☐
8) Give the English for: 'No aguanto a mi tía porque es maleducada.' ☐
9) Translate into English: 'Cumpliré dieciséis años el próximo mes.' ☐
10) How do you say 'He is chatty and sensitive' in Spanish? ☐

Total: ☐

Quiz 4 | Date: ...... / ...... / ......

1) What is 'un bigote' in English? ☐
2) Translate into English: 'Soy hijo único pero tengo muchos amigos.' ☐
3) True or false? The Spanish for 'to get engaged' is 'comprometerse'. ☐
4) Give the Spanish for 'surname'. ☐
5) In Spanish, describe what someone in your family looks like. ☐
6) Translate into English: 'Me relaciono con todos mis parientes.' ☐
7) How do you say 'She is red-haired' in Spanish? ☐
8) Answer this question in Spanish: '¿De dónde eres?' ☐
9) 'Mi padre es gracioso pero serio al mismo tiempo.' Say this in English. ☐
10) Which two nouns mean 'wedding' in Spanish? ☐

Total: ☐

Music

La música

_____ algún instrumento?	Do you play an instrument?
Toco la guitarra en un grupo de rock.	I play _____ in a _____ .
Cuando era pequeño, tocaba _____ y _____ .	When I was little, _____ the piano and the violin.
Canto música clásica en un coro... ...y quiero ser _____ .	I sing classical music in a _____ ... ...and I want to be a singer.
Quiero aprender a tocar la batería... ...pero mi padre no me dejará.	I want to learn to play the _____ ... ...but my father _____ .
Mi hermana _____ y toca _____ en una orquesta.	My sister is a musician and she plays the clarinet in an _____ .

¿Te gusta escuchar música?

Me encanta escuchar ....
porque me hace ....
*I love listening to rap music
because it makes me feel relaxed.*

Escucho muchas grabaciones de
audio de cantantes pop.
*I listen to lots of ....
.... of ....*

.... mi .... preferido es el hip-hop.
I'd say that my favourite genre of music is hip-hop.

Puedo llevar la música conmigo y escucharla cuando salgo
a correr, lo que me parece fenomenal.
*I can take my music with me and ....
while I'm jogging, ...*

Me encanta .... e intento ir a muchos conciertos.
I love live music and I try to go to ....

Sus videos musicales son originales y .... es interesante.
Their .... are original and their lyrics are interesting.

Music

La música

	Do you play an instrument?
	I play the guitar in a rock band.
	When I was little, I used to play the piano and the violin.
	I sing classical music in a choir... ...and I want to be a singer.
	I want to learn to play the drums... ...but my father won't let me.
	My sister is a musician and she plays the clarinet in an orchestra.

¿Te gusta escuchar música?

I love listening to rap music because it makes me feel relaxed.

I listen to lots of audio recordings of pop singers.

I'd say that my favourite genre of music is hip-hop.

I can take my music with me and listen to it while I'm jogging, which seems great to me.

I love live music and I try to go to lots of concerts.

Their music videos are original and their lyrics are interesting.

Topic 3 — Free-Time Activities

 ✓ ✓ ✓

Cinema and TV

En el cine

Me gusta ir .... con mis amigos porque las entradas son baratas.
I like going to the cinema with my friends because ....

Es interesante ver a los actores y .... en sus nuevos papeles.
It's interesting to see the actors and actresses in ....

No me gustan las películas
.... o de ciencia ficción
porque es difícil seguir la trama.
I don't like detective or ....
.... *films because it's*
difficult ....

.... trataba
de un espía. Los efectos especiales y
la banda sonora eran fenomenales.
The action film was about
a spy. The .... *and*
the .... *were great.*

.... la nueva película de terror
porque el reparto está lleno de ....
I'm looking forward to seeing the new ....
.... *because the* .... *is full of stars.*

¿Te gusta ver la tele?

Me gusta ver la tele los sábados.	I like ▮▮▮ on Saturdays.
Mi ▮▮▮ es BBC1...	My favourite channel is BBC1...
...porque no hay anuncios.	...because there aren't any ▮▮▮.
Mucha gente ▮▮▮ que las telenovelas son aburridas...	Many people complain that ▮▮▮ are boring...
...pero no estoy de acuerdo porque me ayudan a ▮▮▮.	...but ▮▮▮ because they help me to relax.
No me gusta ▮▮▮.	I don't like watching the news.
Quisiera ver más ▮▮▮...	I'd like to see more documentaries...
...y menos dibujos animados.	...and fewer ▮▮▮.
Veo ▮▮▮ con mi abuela y participamos juntos.	I watch game shows with my grandma and ▮▮▮.

Cinema and TV

En el cine

I like going to the cinema with my friends because the tickets are cheap.

It's interesting to see the actors and actresses in their new roles.

I don't like detective or science fiction films because it's difficult to follow the plot.

The action film was about a spy. The special effects and the soundtrack were great.

I'm looking forward to seeing the new horror film because the cast is full of stars.

¿Te gusta ver la tele?

	I like watching TV on Saturdays.
	My favourite channel is BBC1... ...because there aren't any adverts.
	Many people complain that soap operas are boring... ...but I don't agree because they help me to relax.
	I don't like watching the news.
	I'd like to see more documentaries... ...and fewer cartoons.
	I watch game shows with my grandma and we join in together.

Topic 3 — Free-Time Activities   ✓ ✓ ✓

Food

Las frutas

la manzana

_____ peach

la fresa

la naranja

_____ banana

la pera

_____ grapes

_____ pineapple

Las verduras

_____ vegetables, pulses

_____ string beans

los champiñones

_____ peas

la zanahoria

la col

_____ onion

la lechuga

Otros alimentos

la carne de vaca

_____ lamb

la carne de cerdo

_____ veal

el pollo

la salchicha

_____ Spanish sausage

el pescado

_____ rice

una barra de pan

_____ cold soup

las tapas

_____ long doughnuts

_____ boiled sweet

el huevo

_____ cream

el aceite

el té

_____ juice

la leche

¿Qué te gusta comer?

Para el desayuno, tomo dos tostadas con _____ y mermelada.
For _____, I have _____ with butter and _____.

_____ a la una. Suelo comer un bocadillo de jamón y queso.
I have lunch at one o'clock. I usually eat _____.

Me tomo _____ con _____ como merienda.
I have a coffee with biscuits as an _____.

Ceno un filete poco hecho con patatas hervidas y _____.
I have _____ with _____ potatoes and roasted garlic for dinner.

Topic 3 — Free-Time Activities

Second Go: ...../...../.....	**Food**

Las frutas

	apple
	peach
	strawberry
	orange
	banana
	pear
	grapes
	pineapple

Las verduras

	vegetables, pulses
	string beans
	mushrooms
	peas
	carrot
	cabbage
	onion
	lettuce

Otros alimentos

	beef		cold soup
	lamb		bar snacks
	pork		long doughnuts
	veal		boiled sweet
	chicken		egg
	sausage		cream
	Spanish sausage		oil
	fish		tea
	rice		juice
	a loaf of bread		milk

¿Qué te gusta comer?

For breakfast, I have two slices of toast with butter and jam.

I have lunch at one o'clock. I usually eat a ham and cheese sandwich.

I have a coffee with biscuits as an afternoon snack.

I have a rare steak with boiled potatoes and roasted garlic for dinner.

Eating Out

First Go:
..... / ..... / .....

¡Vamos al restaurante!

el camarero

waitress

la carta

fork

knife

la cuchara

starter

el segundo plato

(set) dish

la sal

el vaso

la cuenta

la propina

to be thirsty

to be hungry

pepper

drink

included

Me encanta _____ nueva _____, por ejemplo la china o la tailandesa.
I love trying new food, for example _____ or _____.

A veces _____ en restaurantes _____ porque me gustan los
mariscos, especialmente las gambas a la plancha o _____.
Sometimes I have dinner in Mediterranean restaurants because I like
_____, especially _____ or fried squid.

Después de _____ grande, siempre pido algo dulce como _____.
After a big meal, I always _____ something _____ like an ice cream.

¿Qué le gustaría tomar?

Quisiera _____.	I would like a spicy pizza.
Me gustaría la tortilla de champiñones y _____.	_____ the mushroom and a salad.
Para _____, me apetece un pastel.	For dessert, _____ a cake.
Mis abuelos quieren una copa de vino y una cerveza.	My grandparents want _____ and a _____.
Este _____ no es lo que pedí. ¿Me puede _____ el correcto?	This dish isn't _____. Can you bring me the right one?

Topic 3 — Free-Time Activities

Eating Out

¡Vamos al restaurante!

	waiter		to be thirsty
	waitress		to be hungry
	menu		salt
	fork		pepper
	knife		glass
	spoon		drink
	starter		bill
	main course		tip
	(set) dish		included

I love trying new food, for example Chinese or Thai.

Sometimes I have dinner in Mediterranean restaurants because I like seafood, especially grilled prawns or fried squid.

After a big meal, I always order something sweet like an ice cream.

¿Qué le gustaría tomar?

	I would like a spicy pizza.
	I would like the mushroom omelette and a salad.
	For dessert, I fancy a cake.
	My grandparents want a glass of wine and a beer.
	This dish isn't what I ordered. Can you bring me the right one?

Sport

¿Practicas algún deporte?

	horse riding	los deportes de riesgo	
la natación			swimming pool
	sailing		track, court, slope
la pesca		la pista de hielo	
el atletismo			to dance
	mountain climbing	nadar	to
	skating	patinar	to

Mi deporte preferido es...

Me gusta ...	I like riding my bike...
...porque la oportunidad de explorar mi pueblo.	...because it gives me the chance to my town.
tres veces por semana...	I run three times a week...
...y en carreras de 10 km.	...and I take part in .
Me encanta varias veces por semana.	I love going horse riding a week.
Me gusta jugar al bádminton...	I like playing ...
...porque puedo ...	...because I can have fun...
...y hacer deporte .	...and at the same time.
donde practicamos está cerca de mi casa.	The sports centre where is near my house.
No soy exactamente deportista...	I'm not exactly ...
...pero me importa...	...but exercise is important to me...
...ya que mejora .	...as it my mental health.
Voy al colegio y a veces pesco con mi padre...	I go to school by skateboard and sometimes with my father...
...pero prefiero cocinar o leer en mi .	...but I prefer in my free time.

Sport

¿Practicas algún deporte?

	horse riding	adventure sports
	swimming	swimming pool
	sailing	track, court, slope
	fishing	ice rink
	athletics	to dance
	mountain climbing	to swim
	skating	to skate

Mi deporte preferido es...

	I like riding my bike... ...because it gives me the chance to explore my town.
	I run three times a week... ...and I take part in 10 km races.
	I love going horse riding several times a week.
	I like playing badminton... ...because I can have fun... ...and do sport at the same time.
	The sports centre where we practise is near my house.
	I'm not exactly sporty... ...but exercise is important to me... ...as it improves my mental health.
	I go to school by skateboard and sometimes I fish with my father... ...but I prefer to cook or read in my free time.

Topic 3 — Free-Time Activities

Sport

El deporte en directo

Me encantaría visitar un ⬚ ...	to visit a stadium...
...y ⬚ un partido de fútbol.	...and watch a ⬚ .
Me imagino que sería ⬚ ...	I imagine it would be fun...
...si tu equipo marca muchos goles.	...if your team ⬚ lots of ⬚ .
El año pasado, mi ⬚ ganó ⬚ de rugby.	Last year, my favourite team ⬚ the rugby championship.
Fue muy emocionante cuando el capitán alzó ⬚ .	It was very ⬚ when the ⬚ lifted the trophy.

El deporte en la tele

.... al baloncesto. .... ver tantos partidos como sea posible.
I am a fan of .... *. I try to watch* .... *games as possible.*

Prefiero .... que verlo en la tele.
.... pasar mucho tiempo viendo la tele,
pienso que los jóvenes .... practicar deporte.
I prefer playing hockey to .... *.*
Instead of spending a lot of time watching TV,
I think .... *should* .... *.*

Me gusta ver torneos de tenis. Annette Setter es ....
Es una .... impresionante porque casi nunca pierde.
I like watching .... *. Annette Setter is the reigning*
champion. She's an .... *player because she hardly ever* .... *.*

Me encanta ver .... porque es
interesante ver deportes menos populares como el
.... Sueles aprender algo sobre ellos.
I love watching the Olympic Games because
it's interesting to watch .... *like*
canoeing. .... *something about them.*

Sport

El deporte en directo

	I would love to visit a stadium... ...and watch a football match.
	I imagine it would be fun... ...if your team scores lots of goals.
	Last year, my favourite team won the rugby championship.
	It was very exciting when the captain lifted the trophy.

El deporte en la tele

I am a fan of basketball. I try to watch as many games as possible.

I prefer playing hockey to watching it on TV.
Instead of spending a lot of time watching TV,
I think young people should do sport.

I like watching tennis tournaments. Annette Setter is the reigning
champion. She's an impressive player because she hardly ever loses.

I love watching the Olympic Games because
it's interesting to watch less popular sports like
canoeing. You usually learn something about them.

Mixed Practice Quizzes

Well, you've raced through those pages — you must be eager to tackle some quiz questions. Test your knowledge from p.29-40 and add up your scores.

Quiz 1   Date: ...... / ...... / ......

1) Translate into Spanish: 'My grandma used to go horse riding twice a week.'

2) How do you say 'en directo' in English?

3) In Spanish, say what you normally eat for breakfast.

4) How do you say 'Mi padrastro alzará la copa' in English?

5) 'My favourite sport is canoeing because I can have fun with my friends.' Say this in Spanish.

6) Give the Spanish for: 'I was hungry, so I ate a slice of toast.'

7) True or false? 'Una película de acción' means 'a spy film' in English.

8) Translate into Spanish: 'I will listen to music while I'm on the train.'

9) What is the Spanish for 'championship'?

10) Give the English for: 'Suelen comer uvas como merienda.'

Total:

Quiz 2   Date: ...... / ...... / ......

1) 'Normalmente prefiero ver la tele en línea porque hay una gran variedad de programas interesantes.' Say this in English.

2) How would you say 'I used to play the piano and the drums' in Spanish?

3) Give the Spanish for: 'Young people should do more sport.'

4) Translate into English: 'Quisiera un helado, por favor.'

5) Name three types of meat in Spanish.

6) 'El alpinismo es un deporte emocionante.' Say this in English.

7) How do you say 'I fancy a dessert' in Spanish?

8) Translate into Spanish: 'Horror films normally have bad special effects.'

9) True or false? 'Un filete a la plancha' means 'a fried steak'.

10) What is 'la letra de la canción' in English?

Total:

Mixed Practice Quizzes

Quiz 3 Date: ...... / ...... / ......

1) Translate into English: 'Me encantaría ver un partido de baloncesto.'
2) 'We would like to sing in a choir.' Say this in Spanish.
3) How do you say 'una barra de pan' in English?
4) Give the English for: 'Aprendimos algo sobre la vela.'
5) Translate into Spanish: 'My brother used to like watching cartoons.'
6) Answer this question in Spanish:
   '¿Que tipo de deporte te gusta ver en la tele?'
7) 'Me gusta comer un bocadillo de huevo y lechuga.' Say this in English.
8) Translate into Spanish: 'Can you bring me the bill?'
9) How would you say 'el reparto de una película' in English?
10) Give the Spanish for: 'Sport can improve your mental health.'

Total:

Quiz 4 Date: ...... / ...... / ......

1) 'I think game shows are entertaining to watch.' Say this in Spanish.
2) Translate into English: 'Cuando eras niño, comías pescado y arroz.'
3) In Spanish, say what sport you'd do at 'la piscina'.
4) Name three items of cutlery in Spanish.
5) Translate into English: 'Fue a todos los conciertos de su grupo preferido.'
6) Give the English for: 'Mi hermana fue aficionada al atletismo.'
7) True or false? The Spanish for 'boiled peas' is 'los guisantes hervidos'.
8) What is 'una tortilla de queso y cebolla' in English?
9) How would you say 'I didn't like the plot' in Spanish?
10) Translate into English: 'Prefiero jugar al bádminton que
    verlo en la tele porque me gusta hacer ejercicio.'

Total:

Technology

La tecnología

Mi madre usa ▮▮▮▮▮ para descargar canciones.	My mum uses the computer to ▮▮▮▮▮ .
▮▮▮▮▮ un portátil para hacer mis deberes.	I use a ▮▮▮▮▮ to do my homework.
¿Para qué usas tu ▮▮▮▮▮ ?	What do you use your mobile for?
Sin mi móvil, ▮▮▮▮▮ ...	Without my mobile, I couldn't...
...ni mandar ni ▮▮▮▮▮ mensajes.	... ▮▮▮▮▮ or receive messages.
...hablar con mis amigos.	... ▮▮▮▮▮ to my friends.

La red

Me encanta .... por la red y creo
que es crucial para la vida moderna.
*I love surfing the .... and I
think it's crucial for ....*

Es mucho más cómodo
hacer las compras ....
*It's a lot more ....
to do your shopping online.*

.... es una herramienta muy útil porque puedes
usar .... para encontrar información.
*The Internet is a very useful .... because you can
use a search engine to ....*

Me gustan .... porque puedes comunicarte con otros usuarios.
I like video games because you can .... with other ....

Muchos .... usan la red para sus cuentas
bancarias porque .... ir al banco.
*Many Internet users use the web for their ....
.... because it's easier than going to the bank.*

Leo los correos electrónicos en un .... en lugar de una aplicación.
I read .... in a browser instead of an ....

Second Go:
..... / ..... / .....

Technology

La tecnología

	My mum uses the computer to download songs. 
	I use a laptop to do my homework.
	What do you use your mobile for?
	Without my mobile, I couldn't... ...send or receive messages. ...talk to my friends.

La red

I love surfing the Internet and I think it's crucial for modern life.

It's a lot more convenient to do your shopping online.

The Internet is a very useful tool because you can use a search engine to find information.

I like video games because you can communicate with other users.

Many Internet users use the web for their bank accounts because it's easier than going to the bank.

I read emails in a browser instead of an application.

Technology

Lo malo de la tecnología

Lo peor de los móviles es que la gente puede .... sin
informarte y compartir tus fotos con otra gente ....
.... *about mobiles is that people can record videos without*
telling you and .... *with other people you don't know.*

.... es cuando mis amigos se enfadan
porque no contesto a sus .... enseguida.
The most irritating thing is when my friends ....
because I don't .... *to their messages* ....

No puedes .... de la tecnología. Siempre tienes que estar conectado.
You can't escape from .... *You always have* ....

Creo que la tecnología puede ....
Es importante desconectarse ....
I think that technology can be addictive.
It's important to .... *from time to time.*

Protegerse en línea

Hay que .... tu identidad con una contraseña segura.	You must protect your identity with ....
Si alguien averigua tu	If someone .... your password...
...puede .... a tus archivos...	...they can access your ....
...y .... tu disco duro.	...and ruin your ....
También deberías .... el correo basura del	You should also delete .... from your inbox...
...porque la gente puede adjuntar	...because people can .... a virus...
...que daña tu	...that .... your computer.
Un buen servidor de seguridad te protegerá de estas amenazas.	A good .... will protect you from these ....

Topic 4 — Technology in Everyday Life

Technology

Lo malo de la tecnología

The worst thing about mobiles is that people can record videos without telling you and share your photos with other people you don't know.

The most irritating thing is when my friends get angry because I don't reply to their messages straightaway.

You can't escape from technology. You always have to be connected.

I think that technology can be addictive.
It's important to disconnect from time to time.

Protegerse en línea

	You must protect your identity with a strong password.
	If someone finds out your password... ...they can access your files... ...and ruin your hard disk.
	You should also delete spam from your inbox... ...because people can attach a virus... ...that harms your computer.
	A good firewall will protect you from these threats.

Topic 4 — Technology in Everyday Life

 ✓ ✓ ✓

Social Media

Las redes sociales

Uso _____ para...	I use social networks to...
...charlar con mis primos en India.	... ____ with my cousins in India.
...compartir fotos con mis amigos.	... ____ photos with my friends.
...leer ____ sobre mis intereses.	...read blogs about my interests.
...colgar recetas en algunos ____ .	... ____ recipes on some websites.
... ____ sobre música.	...watch videos about music.

Mis padres _____ de las redes sociales ya que no las entienden.
My parents are scared of social networks ____ they don't _____ them.

Las ventajas y desventajas

_____ las redes sociales, sé lo que está pasando en el mundo.
Thanks to social networks, I know _____ in the world.

No te aburres nunca y siempre hay _____.
You never _____ and there's always something to do.

Es muy fácil _____ con los amigos pero es importante salir con ellos también.
It's very easy to keep in contact with your friends but it's important _____ too.

_____, siempre hay alguien con quien puedo _____. Por otra parte, las salas de chat pueden ser peligrosas.
On one hand, there's always someone I can chat to. On the other hand, _____ can be _____.

Debido a las redes sociales, _____ mirando cosas inútiles.
_____ social networks, I waste time looking at ____ things.

La gente te puede ____. Por eso, voy a ____ mi cuenta.
People can lie to you. Therefore, I'm going to deactivate my ____.

_____ la gente pasa demasiado tiempo en las redes sociales.
I would say that people _____ on social networks.

Social Media

Las redes sociales

	I use social networks to...
	...chat with my cousins in India.
	...share photos with my friends.
	...read blogs about my interests.
	...post recipes on some websites.
	...watch videos about music.

My parents are scared of social networks as they don't understand them.

Las ventajas y desventajas

Thanks to social networks, I know what's happening in the world.

You never get bored and there's always something to do.

It's very easy to keep in contact with your friends but it's important to go out with them too.

On one hand, there's always someone I can chat to. On the other hand, chat rooms can be dangerous.

Due to social networks, I waste time looking at useless things.

People can lie to you. Therefore, I'm going to deactivate my account.

I would say that people spend too much time on social networks.

Mixed Practice Quizzes

I checked my notifications and it looks like there are some quizzes ready to test your knowledge of p.43-48. Technology — it's the gift that keeps on giving.

Quiz 1 Date: ...... / ...... / ......

1) What is the English for 'el portátil'?

2) Translate into Spanish: 'I like recording music with my friends.'

3) Give the English for: 'Mi hermana veía vídeos sobre los videojuegos.'

4) True or false? The English for 'una contraseña' is 'hard disk'.

5) In Spanish, give two things you might use a mobile for.

6) Translate into English: 'Carlos se mantuvo en contacto con sus primos.'

7) How do you say 'search engine' in Spanish?

8) Translate into Spanish: 'Many people are scared of social networks.'

9) 'A mi abuelo le gusta navegar por la red.' Say this in English.

10) In Spanish, give two disadvantages of technology.

Total:

Quiz 2 Date: ...... / ...... / ......

1) Give two Spanish verbs that mean 'to send'.

2) Translate into English: 'Siempre estoy conectada.'

3) How do you say 'to do online shopping' in Spanish?

4) In Spanish, give two advantages of social networks.

5) What is the Spanish for a 'firewall'?

6) How do you say 'colgar una foto' in English?

7) Give the English for: 'Mi tío escribirá un blog sobre la cocina.'

8) Answer this question in Spanish: '¿Para qué usas un ordenador?'

9) Translate into English: 'La tecnología es una adicción.'

10) What is the English for 'desconectarse'?

Total:

50

Mixed Practice Quizzes

Quiz 3 | Date: ...... / ...... / ......

1) True or false? 'Charlar' means 'to chat' in English.

2) Translate into English: 'Usaron un navegador para leer las noticias.'

3) 'You can't always reply to messages straightaway.' Say this in Spanish.

4) What is the English for 'adjuntar un archivo'?

5) How do you say 'inbox' in Spanish?

6) Translate into Spanish: 'Sometimes I want to escape from technology.'

7) 'Diría que las salas de chat son demasiado peligrosas.' Say this in English.

8) Give the Spanish for 'Internet user'.

9) 'The worst thing about social networks is that people can lie to you.'
Translate this sentence into Spanish.

10) How do you say 'el correo basura' in English?

Total:

Quiz 4 | Date: ...... / ...... / ......

1) Give the English for: 'Alguien compartió las fotos de mi amigo.'

2) Translate into Spanish: 'Thanks to social networks, I never get bored.'

3) How do you say 'to download songs' in Spanish?

4) Give the English for: 'Mi padre usa la red para su cuenta bancaria.'

5) 'It's crucial to know what's happening in the world.' Say this in Spanish.

6) Translate into English: 'Es importante proteger tu identidad en línea.'

7) How do you say 'una aplicación' in English?

8) 'Da dos desventajas de las redes sociales.'
Give your answer in Spanish.

9) What is the English for 'una herramienta útil'?

10) Give the English for: 'I prefer going out with my friends
instead of spending lots of time on the Internet.'

Total:

Customs and Festivals

First Go:
..... / ..... / .....

¡Celebremos!

¡Feliz cumpleaños! ⬜

⬜ Congratulations!

¡Feliz año nuevo! ⬜

⬜ New Year

tener suerte ⬜

⬜ to celebrate

⬜ public holiday

el santo ⬜

En Argentina, se celebra _____ el 9 de julio.
In Argentina, national independence day _____ on 9th July.

'La Tomatina' tiene lugar en agosto en Buñol, Valencia
y atrae a miles de turistas. _____
se lanzan tomates _____ .
*'La Tomatina' _____ in August in Buñol, Valencia
and _____ of tourists. Participants
throw tomatoes at each other.*

En _____ en España, _____ 12 uvas para traer buena suerte.
On New Year's Eve in Spain, 12 grapes are eaten to bring _____ .

San Fermín

The running of the bulls happens
at the festival of San Fermín.

Muchas personas _____ por las calles estrechas de
Pamplona con _____ hasta la plaza de toros.
*Many people run through the _____ streets of
Pamplona with the dangerous bulls to the _____ .*

Los habitantes y _____ llevan ropa blanca y pañuelos rojos.
_____ *and tourists wear white clothes and _____ .*

_____ es una tradición
común en España, y _____ son
admirados por muchas personas.
*Bullfighting is a _____
in Spain, and bullfighters are
_____ by many people.*

Es polémica porque _____
_____ piensa que es _____
matar animales por diversión.
*It is _____ because
some people think that it's
cruel to kill animals _____ .*

Second Go:
..... / ..... / .....

Customs and Festivals

¡Celebremos!

Happy Birthday!

Congratulations!

Happy New Year!

New Year

to be lucky

to celebrate

public holiday

saint's day

In Argentina, national independence day is celebrated on 9th July.

'La Tomatina' takes place in August in Buñol, Valencia and attracts thousands of tourists. Participants throw tomatoes at each other.

On New Year's Eve in Spain, 12 grapes are eaten to bring good luck.

San Fermín

The .... happens at the festival of San Fermín.

Many people run through the narrow streets of Pamplona with the dangerous bulls to the bullring.

Locals and tourists wear white clothes and red scarves.

Bullfighting is a common tradition in Spain, and bullfighters are admired by many people.

It is controversial because some people think that it's cruel to kill animals for fun.

 ☑ ☑ ☑

Customs and Festivals

El Día de los Muertos

La gente cree que .... reciben .... para regresar durante 24 horas.
People .... the dead receive permission to .... for 24 hours.

El Día de los Muertos (...........................) is celebrated in ...., Central America and the Philippines and begins at .... on 1st November.

En la tradición mexicana, ... no es aterradora y .... las vidas de los muertos.
In ...., death isn't .... and .... of the dead are celebrated.

'la Catrina' is a popular female skeleton icon.

Alguna gente lleva maquillaje como y _____ de 'la Catrina'.	Some people wear _____ like and dress up as 'la Catrina'.
_____ a los muertos con calaveras de azúcar, _____ y música del mariachi.	They honour the dead with _____, flowers and _____.
Las familias limpian y arreglan las _____ de sus _____ y amigos.	Families _____ and _____ the graves of their relatives and friends.

El Día de los Inocentes

El Día de los Inocentes se celebra ....
El Día de los Inocentes is celebrated on 28th December.

Es un día lleno de bromas.	It's a day _____.
Es tradicional gastar una broma a alguien, por ejemplo...	It's traditional to _____ on someone, for example...
...sustituir el azúcar por la sal.	... _____ sugar with salt.
... _____ la hora _____.	...change the time on the clock.
Los medios de comunicación presentan _____ de _____.	The _____ feature false news stories as a joke.

Customs and Festivals

El Día de los Muertos

People believe the dead receive permission to return for 24 hours.

.... (All Souls' Day) is celebrated in ....,' .... and .... and begins at midnight on ....

In Mexican tradition, death isn't frightening and the lives of the dead are celebrated.

'..............................' is a popular female skeleton icon.

	Some people wear make-up like and dress up as 'la Catrina'.
	They honour the dead with sugar skulls, flowers and Mexican music.
	Families clean and tidy the graves of their relatives and friends.

El Día de los Inocentes

El Día de los Inocentes is celebrated on 28th December.

	It's a day full of jokes.
	It's traditional to play a joke on someone, for example... ...substitute sugar with salt. ...change the time on the clock.
	The media feature false news stories as a joke.

Topic 5 — Customs and Festivals

Customs and Festivals

Semana Santa

La Pascua es un evento sombrío con muchas ....
.... is a event with a lot of customs.

La gente enciende velas en la iglesia durante ....
People .... in .... during Easter Mass.

Durante la Semana Santa, hay .... con música.
During ...., there are processions with music.

.... por las calles y la gente lleva ropa que esconde sus identidades.
Statues are carried around the streets and people wear clothes that ....

¡Feliz Navidad!

Me encanta cantar ...	I love singing Christmas carols...
...y me gusta comer turrón.	...and I like to eat .
trae regalos a los niños.	Father Christmas brings the children .
En España, se celebra la Nochebuena...	In Spain, is celebrated...
...con .	...with a big family dinner.
celebran el Día de Reyes el 6 de enero.	Many Spaniards celebrate on 6th January.

Otras fiestas religiosas

Durante ...., muchos musulmanes ayunan durante las horas de luz.
During Ramadan, many Muslims .... during ....
El Eid al-Fitr es una .... que marca el fin del mes de Ramadán.
Eid al-Fitr is a Muslim festival that .... of the month of Ramadan.

Muchos .... celebran Hanukkah. Lo festejan durante ocho días.
Many Jews celebrate Hanukkah. They .... it for eight days.
Se encienden velas, se dan regalos y se comen ....
..............., gifts are .... and fried food is eaten.

Customs and Festivals

Semana Santa

Easter is a sombre event
with a lot of customs.

People light candles in church
during Easter Mass.

During Holy Week, there are
processions with music.

Statues are carried around the streets and
people wear clothes that hide their identities.

¡Feliz Navidad!

	I love singing Christmas carols... ...and I like to eat nougat.
	Father Christmas brings the children presents.
	In Spain, Christmas Eve is celebrated... ...with a big family dinner.
	Many Spaniards celebrate Epiphany on 6th January.

Otras fiestas religiosas

During Ramadan, many Muslims fast during daylight hours.

Eid al-Fitr is a Muslim festival that marks the end of the month of Ramadan.

Many Jews celebrate Hanukkah. They celebrate it for eight days.

Candles are lit, gifts are given and fried food is eaten.

Mixed Practice Quizzes

Right, it's time to follow tradition and tackle some customary quizzes. See what you can remember from p.51-56 and tot up your scores at the end.

Quiz 1   Date: ...... / ...... / ......

1) Translate into English: 'La corrida de toros es polémica.'

2) Give two Spanish verbs that mean 'to celebrate'.

3) What is the Spanish for 'to play a joke'?

4) Translate into Spanish: 'We always used to sing Christmas carols.'

5) Give the English for: 'El Eid al-Fitr marca el fin de Ramadán.'

6) How do you say 'Happy Birthday!' in Spanish?

7) Give the Spanish for 'Holy Week'.

8) Give the English for 'las calaveras de azúcar'.

9) 'Sus padres limpiaron las tumbas de sus parientes.' Say this in English.

10) What is the Spanish for 'good luck'?

Total:

Quiz 2   Date: ...... / ...... / ......

1) 'Se cree que los muertos regresan durante 24 horas.'
    Translate this sentence into English.

2) Give the Spanish for 'public holiday'.

3) Give the English for: '¡Feliz año nuevo!'

4) Answer this question in Spanish: '¿Qué hace Papá Noel?'

5) Translate into English: 'Algunas personas se disfrazan de 'la Catrina'.'

6) Give the Spanish for: 'Gifts are given during Hanukkah.'

7) True or false? 'La Tomatina' takes place in Buñol.

8) What is 'la plaza de toros' in English?

9) When is 'El Día de los Inocentes' celebrated?

10) In Spanish, give one thing that happens during Easter Mass.

Total:

Mixed Practice Quizzes

Quiz 3   Date: ...... / ...... / ......

1) Translate into English: 'Se celebran Hanukkah durante ocho días.'
2) What is 'iFelicitaciones!' in English?
3) 'The media also take part in 'El Día de los Inocentes'.' Say this in Spanish.
4) True or false? Many Spaniards celebrate Epiphany.
5) How many grapes are eaten for luck on New Year's Eve in Spain?
6) How would you say 'la música del mariachi' in English?
7) Translate into Spanish: 'I don't like bullfighting because I think it's cruel.'
8) Give the Spanish for: 'People carry statues around the streets.'
9) Give the English for: 'Se honra a los difuntos en la tradición mexicana.'
10) How do you say 'customs' in Spanish?

Total:

Quiz 4   Date: ...... / ...... / ......

1) Translate into English: 'Mucha gente admira a los toreros.'
2) How do you say 'Easter Mass' in Spanish?
3) Translate into Spanish: 'Many Muslims will fast during Ramadan.'
4) In Spanish, give one joke people might play on 'El Día de los Inocentes'.
5) Give the English for 'la fecha patria'.
6) What is the Spanish for 'Christmas Eve'?
7) Translate into English: 'Celebramos con una gran cena familiar.'
8) How do you say 'saint's day' in Spanish?
9) In Spanish, say when 'El Día de los Muertos' takes place.
10) What is the Spanish for 'New Year's Eve'?

Total:

Topic 5 — Customs and Festivals

Talking About Where You Live

First Go:
..... / ..... / .....

¿Dónde vives?

las afueras			market
	port / harbour	la peluquería	
el ayuntamiento			butcher's
el aparcamiento		el estanco	
	park		book shop
la mezquita		la pastelería	
la biblioteca			fishmonger's
	factory	la panadería	
la comisaría			stationery shop
	theatre	Correos	

Vivo ⬚ una ciudad.	I live near ⬚ .
Vivo en ⬚ .	I live in a really small town.
Preferiría vivir más cerca del ⬚ ...	⬚ closer to the sea...
...porque ⬚ la vela.	...because I love sailing.

Háblame de tu pueblo

Creo que .... en el campo que ....
I think it's better to live .... than in the city.

Mi ciudad tiene ....
También hay un museo impresionante ....
My city has various pretty buildings. There's
also .... in the centre.

\\\|/////|||||||||/|//,
'tuviera' is the
imperfect subjunctive
of '............................'.
/////|||||||\\\\/////|\\\

Mi barrio .... si tuviera una bolera.
.... *would be almost perfect if it had ....*

.... , viviría lejos del
centro comercial porque ....
In an ideal world, I'd live far away from ....
.... *because there are so many people.*

Talking About Where You Live

¿Dónde vives?

	outskirts		market
	port / harbour		hairdresser's
	town hall		butcher's
	parking		tobacconist's
	park		book shop
	mosque		pastry shop
	library		fishmonger's
	factory		bakery
	police station		stationery shop
	theatre		Post Office

	I live near a city.
	I live in a really small town.
	I'd prefer to live closer to the sea... ...because I love sailing.

Háblame de tu pueblo

I think it's better to live in the countryside than in the city.

My city has various pretty buildings. There's also an impressive museum in the centre.

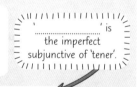

'........................' is the imperfect subjunctive of 'tener'.

My neighbourhood would be almost perfect if it had a bowling alley.

In an ideal world, I'd live far away from the shopping centre because there are so many people.

Topic 6 — Where You Live

 ☑ ☑ ☑

The Home

Mi casa

la planta baja

la segunda planta

el sótano

_____ stairs

el comedor

el suelo

la pared

bathroom

carpet

to move house

Vivo en ....
I live in a semi-detached house.

Vivimos en un piso pequeño.
We live in ....

Hay siete habitaciones en mi casa.
There are .... in my house.

La habitación que ....
.... es el salón porque
hay sillones cómodos y
.... llena de libros.
The room I like best is the ....
because there are ....
armchairs and shelves ....

En mi casa, ...	In my house, there's little furniture.
Hay una ducha y un aseo.	There's .... and ....
..............................., hay...	In my bedroom, ...
..............................., un armario, un espejo y	...a bed, ..., and a little table.
En la cocina, hay...	..............................., there is...
...un fregadero, ..., un microondas y	..., a fridge, and an oven.

Mi casa ideal

.... tendría muchos .... y un jardín grande.
My ideal house .... lots of electrical appliances and ....

La casa de mis sueños tendría .... de lujo.
Además, sería mejor .... mi habitación.
The house .... would have a luxury pool.
.... if I didn't have to share my room.

The Home

Mi casa

	ground floor		bathroom
	second floor		floor
	basement		carpet
	stairs		wall
	dining room		to move house

I live in a semi-detached house.

We live in a small flat.

There are seven rooms in my house.

The room I like best is the lounge because there are comfortable armchairs and shelves full of books.

	In my house, there's little furniture.
	There's a shower and a toilet.
	In my bedroom, there is... ...a bed, a wardrobe, a mirror and a little table.
	In the kitchen, there is... ...a sink, a fridge, a microwave and an oven.

Mi casa ideal

My ideal house would have lots of electrical appliances and a big garden.

The house of my dreams would have a luxury pool.
It would also be better if I didn't have to share my room.

What You Do at Home

Un día típico

¿Qué haces .... ?
What .... in the morning?

⟵

.... verbs let you say what you do to yourself.

Me pongo la bufanda.
.... my scarf.

....
He/She puts on make up.

.... a las siete y luego me ducho.
I wake up at seven o'clock and then ....

.... hasta las siete y media. Luego .... y me visto rápidamente.
I don't get up .... Then I wash my face and .... quickly.

.... a las diez pero no me duermo hasta las once.
I go to bed at ten but .... until eleven.

Las tareas domésticas

Cada mañana, [____] ... ...y arreglo mi dormitorio.	Every morning, I make my bed... ...and [____] .
[____] , quito la mesa... ...y [____] .	After eating, [____] ... ...and I wash the dishes.
En el verano, corto el césped.	In the summer, [____] .
[____] todos los lunes.	I take the rubbish out [____] .
Espero que [____] en casa.	I hope that everyone helps at home.
No me dejan poner la mesa... ...porque siempre [____] .	They don't let me [____] ... ...because I always break something.
Limpio el salón [____] .	[____] on Sundays.
Me gusta pasar la aspiradora.	I like [____] .
[____] los sábados.	We do the shopping on Saturdays.
Paseo al perro después del colegio.	[____] after school.

What You Do at Home

Un día típico

What do you do in the morning?

Reflexive verbs let you say
.

I put on my scarf.

I wake up at seven o'clock and then I have a shower.

He/She puts on make up.

I don't get up until half past seven. Then I wash my face and get dressed quickly.

I go to bed at ten but I don't go to sleep until eleven.

Las tareas domésticas

	Every morning, I make my bed... ...and I tidy my bedroom.
	After eating, I clear the table... ...and I wash the dishes.
	In the summer, I mow the lawn.
	I take the rubbish out every Monday.
	I hope that everyone helps at home.
	They don't let me lay the table... ...because I always break something.
	I clean the lounge on Sundays.
	I like doing the vacuuming.
	We do the shopping on Saturdays.
	I walk the dog after school.

Mixed Practice Quizzes

You're starting to make yourself at home with these topics now. Use these
questions to check what you remember from p.59-64, then add up your scores.

Quiz 1   Date: ...... / ...... / ......

1) Translate into English: 'En el comedor, hay una mesa grande.'

2) 'We used to live in a city, but now we live near the coast.'
   Say this in Spanish.

3) True or false? Reflexive verbs show what you do to other people.

4) How do you say 'shelves' in Spanish?

5) In Spanish, say how many rooms you have at home.

6) Give the English for: 'Paso la aspiradora los jueves.'

7) What is 'la librería' in English?

8) How do you say 'to take out the rubbish' in Spanish?

9) Translate into English: 'Hay una mezquita bonita en mi barrio.'

10) Give the English for: 'Me lavo la cara antes de acostarme.'

Total:

Quiz 2   Date: ...... / ...... / ......

1) In Spanish, say what type of home you live in.

2) Give the English for: 'Me encanta pasear al perro.'

3) Answer this question in Spanish: '¿Te gusta donde vives?'

4) Translate into English: 'Hay tres dormitorios y un cuarto de baño.'

5) What does 'vestirse por la mañana' mean in English?

6) What does 'Había tanta gente en la pescadería' mean in English?

7) True or false? 'To clear the table' is 'poner la mesa' in Spanish.

8) Give the English for:
   'Preferiría vivir en el campo porque sería más tranquilo.'

9) How do you say 'Nos levantamos a las seis y media' in English?

10) Name three pieces of furniture in Spanish.

Total:

Mixed Practice Quizzes

Quiz 3   Date: ...... / ...... / ......

1) How do you say 'Correos' in English?
2) What is 'la tercera planta' in English?
3) 'They loved living in the city centre because there was lots to do.' Say this in Spanish.
4) Give the English for: 'Lavo los platos cada día.'
5) Translate into English: 'En un mundo ideal, viviría cerca de una pastelería.'
6) 'My parents used to do all the shopping, but now I help.' Say this in Spanish.
7) What is the Spanish for 'My aunt lives in a town'?
8) True or false? 'Despertarse' means 'to get up'.
9) Give the English for: 'Hay muchos muebles en el sótano.'
10) Answer this question in Spanish: '¿Cómo sería tu casa ideal?'

Total:

Quiz 4   Date: ...... / ...... / ......

1) Translate into English: 'No me gusta hacer la cama.'
2) How do you say 'No hay escalera en nuestra casa' in English?
3) Translate into Spanish: 'There are lots of factories in my town.'
4) 'Mañana me ducharé a las seis porque tendré que salir temprano.' Say this in English.
5) In Spanish, say what appliances are in your kitchen.
6) What is the English for 'el aparcamiento en el centro de la ciudad'?
7) Give the Spanish for: 'I moved house last year.'
8) Give the English for 'arreglar' and 'limpiar'.
9) 'There aren't many electrical appliances in our house.' Say this in Spanish.
10) What is 'la peluquería' in English?

Total:

Clothes Shopping

De compras

los grandes almacenes ....

la joyería ....

.... to be in fashion

.... designer clothes

los probadores ....

las rebajas ....

la falda ....

.... shirt

la camiseta ....

.... jeans

la rebeca ....

.... socks

Este vestido ....
Quisiera que ....
This .... is too big for me.
.... you to change it for me.

Estoy buscando unos pendientes,
pero no quiero ....
I'm looking for .... ,
but I don't want to spend too much.

Quisiera un collar y un bolso que ....
I'd like .... and .... which aren't expensive.

.... un regalo para mi hermana, así que fui a la zapatería.
I had to buy a present for my sister, so I went to ....

Ya que no había .... , fui a otra
tienda para comprarle una chaqueta de cuero.
As there weren't any trainers, I went to another shop to buy her ....

Me gustaría...

Me encanta .... abrigo.
I love that .... over there.

¿Me lo puedo probar?
Can I .... ?

¿Hay .... ?
Is there another size?

Me gustaría ....
I would like this tie.

Creo que me quedaría bien.
I think ....

Devoluciones y quejas

.... salesperson

el/la dependiente/a ....

a mitad de precio ....

.... discount

quejarse ....

.... to queue

devolver ....

.... to refund

.... to be ripped

estar roto/a ....

.... a hole

una mancha ....

Clothes Shopping

De compras

.... department store

.... jeweller's

.... to be in fashion

.... designer clothes

.... changing rooms

.... the sales

.... skirt

.... shirt

.... T-shirt

.... jeans

.... cardigan

.... socks

This dress is too big for me.
I'd like you to change it for me.

I'm looking for some earrings,
but I don't want to spend too much.

I'd like a necklace and a bag which aren't expensive.

I had to buy a present for my sister, so I went to the shoe shop.

As there weren't any trainers, I went to another shop to buy her a leather jacket.

Me gustaría...

I love that coat over there.

Can I try it on?

Is there another size?

I would like this tie.

I think it would suit me.

Devoluciones y quejas

.... salesperson

.... sales assistant

.... half-price

.... discount

.... to complain

.... to queue

.... to return

.... to refund

.... to be ripped

.... to be broken

.... a hole

.... a stain

More Shopping

En la tienda de comestibles

pagar

cash

la caja

receipt

la cantidad

una lata

cashier

carton

piece

jar

lleno/a

vacío/a

Quisiera ___ de tarta...	I would like a slice of cake...
...y una ración de queso de cabra.	...and ___ of goat's cheese.
¿ ___ una caja?	How much does ___ cost?
Necesitamos ___ de patatas.	___ a bag of potatoes.
Nos hacen falta unos tomates.	___ some tomatoes.
¿Puede usted pesar estas peras?	Could you ___ these pears?
___ de naranjas...	Give me two kilos of oranges...
...y doscientos gramos de harina.	...and ___ of flour.
¿ ___ con tarjeta de crédito?	Can I pay ___ ?

¿Te gusta hacer las compras en la red?

___ es fácil y resulta más barato. Además, no tienes que salir de casa porque hay un servicio de reparto a domicilio.
Shopping online is easy and ___ .
___ , *you don't have to leave the house because there's* ___ .

Prefiero ___ en un centro comercial porque para mí, ___ ver las cosas antes de comprarlas.
I prefer to go shopping in a ___ *because, for me, it's better to see things* ___ *them.*

Use 'antes de' and the infinitive to say ' ___ '.
Use 'después de' and the infinitive to say ' ___ '.

More Shopping

En la tienda de comestibles

	to pay		cashier		piece
	cash		quantity		jar
	till		carton		full
	receipt		tin		empty

	I would like a slice of cake... ...and a portion of goat's cheese.
	How much does a box cost?
	We need a bag of potatoes.
	We need some tomatoes.
	Could you weigh these pears?
	Give me two kilos of oranges... ...and two hundred grams of flour.
	Can I pay by credit card?

¿Te gusta hacer las compras en la red?

Shopping online is easy and turns out cheaper. Besides, you don't have to leave the house because there's a home delivery service.

I prefer to go shopping in a shopping centre because, for me, it's better to see things before buying them.

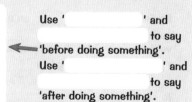

Use ' ' and to say 'before doing something'.

Use ' ' and to say 'after doing something'.

Giving and Asking for Directions

¿Dónde está?

El banco está ____ .	____ is at the end of the street.
____ está justo al lado de la piscina, ____ .	The bakery is ____ the swimming pool, opposite the cinema.
____ detrás del museo.	It's situated ____ the museum.
Los servicios están ____ .	____ are on the corner.
Está delante de ____ .	It is ____ the Post Office.

Es ____ encontrarlo/la.
It's very easy ____ .

Es ____ verlo/la.
It's quite difficult ____ .

> Use the verb 'estar' to describe ____ . You can also use 'estar situado' to say ____ .

¿Cómo se llega a...?

____ y el ayuntamiento está entre ____ y la biblioteca.
Continue straight on and the ____ is ____ the cathedral and the ____ .

> Use the '____' form of the imperative to give instructions or directions to someone you don't know.

____ y verá un semáforo. Luego gire a la izquierda. El parque ____ del colegio.
Take that road and you'll see ____ . ____ . The park is on the right of the school.

____ , tome la primera salida. ____ está a la izquierda.
At the roundabout, ____ . The post box is on the left.

Tome la segunda calle a la derecha. Siga todo recto y ____ .
Take ____ on the right. Continue straight on and cross the street.

Giving and Asking for Directions

¿Dónde está?

	The bank is at the end of the street.
	The bakery is right next to the swimming pool, opposite the cinema.
	It's situated behind the museum.
	The toilets are on the corner.
	It is in front of the Post Office.

It's very easy to find it.

It's quite difficult to see it.

Use the verb ' .... ' to describe where things are. You can also use ' .... ' to say where something is situated.

¿Cómo se llega a...?

Use the ' .... ' form of the .... to give instructions or directions to someone you don't know.

Continue straight on and the town hall is between the cathedral and the library.

Take that road and you'll see some traffic lights. Then turn left. The park is on the right of the school.

At the roundabout, take the first exit. The post box is on the left.

Take the second street on the right. Continue straight on and cross the street.

Weather

Hace buen / mal tiempo

Está...

.... _clear_

nublado

.... _raining_

nevando

.... _hot_

fresco .... _humid_

tormentoso .... _dry_

.... _sol_

calor

.... _It's..._

.... _windy_

.... _cold_

.... _There is / there are..._

niebla ....

ice

.... _showers_

tormenta ....

En ...., hace buen tiempo.
In summer, ...

En el otoño, hace ....
..............., _the weather is bad._

.... es húmedo en primavera.
The climate .... _in_ ....

Nevará en Inglaterra este ....
.... _in England this winter._

Consultaré ....
I will check the weather forecast.

¿Qué tiempo habrá?

Estará fresco .	everywhere.
Hoy el cielo .	Today the sky will be cloudy.
Hará mucho calor en .	in the south.
Sería mejor si no hiciera ... ...porque prefiero el frío.	It would be better if it weren't so hot... ...because .
Hoy en el sur, pero mañana cambiará.	Today it's really sunny in the south, but tomorrow .
Habrá y relámpagos.	There will be thunder and .
Mañana hará sol con .	Tomorrow with the chance of rain.

 ✓ ✓ ✓

Topic 6 — Where You Live

Second Go:
..... / ..... / .....

Weather

Hace buen / mal tiempo

....	_It's..._	....	hot	....	_It's..._
....	clear	....	fresh	....	sunny
....	cloudy	....	humid	....	windy
....	raining	....	stormy	....	hot
....	snowing	....	dry	....	cold

....	_There is / there are..._
....	fog
....	ice
....	a storm
....	showers

In summer, the weather is good.

In autumn, the weather is bad.

The climate is humid in spring.

It will snow in England this winter.

I will check the weather forecast.

¿Qué tiempo habrá?

	It will be fresh everywhere.
	Today the sky will be cloudy.
	It will be very hot in the south.
	It would be better if it weren't so hot... ...because I prefer the cold.
	Today it's really sunny in the south, but tomorrow it will change.
	There will be thunder and lightning.
	Tomorrow it will be sunny with the chance of rain.

Mixed Practice Quizzes

After browsing through p.67-74, you'll want to test your knowledge on shopping, directions and weather. Try these questions and tot up your score for each quiz.

Quiz 1   Date: ...... / ...... / ......

1) Translate into English: '¿Cuánto cuestan dos pedazos?'

2) Mika went shopping and bought 'un collar' and 'unos pendientes'. Which shop did they visit?

3) Give the Spanish for: 'The toilets are next to the shop.'

4) How would you ask if you can try on a shirt in Spanish?

5) True or false? 'Frío' means 'fresh' in English.

6) Give the English for: 'Hace sol en el verano.'

7) In Spanish, ask if you can pay in cash, then ask for a receipt.

8) What are 'los chubascos' in English?

9) Give two words in Spanish for someone who works in a shop.

10) Give the English for: 'Siga todo recto. El museo está en la esquina.'

Total:

Quiz 2   Date: ...... / ...... / ......

1) Give the English for: 'Prefiere hacer las compras en la red.'

2) True or false? 'Gire a la derecha' means 'Turn left'.

3) Give the Spanish for: 'I would like these jeans.'

4) Translate into English: 'Normalmente el clima es seco.'

5) What are 'las rebajas' in English?

6) Translate into Spanish: 'Me hace falta una lata de tomates.'

7) In Spanish, describe where your school is.

8) Translate into English: 'Quisiera que me reembolse.'

9) In Spanish, give three weather phrases that use 'está'.

10) 'Take the third exit at the roundabout. Continue straight on, then take the second street on the left.' Say this in Spanish.

Total:

Mixed Practice Quizzes

Quiz 3 Date: ...... / ...... / ......

1) In Spanish, give two reasons you might return an item of clothing.
2) Give the Spanish for: 'That box is empty.'
3) What is 'weather forecast' in Spanish?
4) Give the English for: 'El banco está detrás del castillo.'
5) Translate into English: 'Fuisteis a los grandes almacenes.'
6) How do you say 'enfrente de' in English?
7) 'Voy a consultar, pero pienso que hará mucho viento mañana por la tarde.' Say this in English.
8) Give the Spanish for: 'This dress does not suit me.'
9) In Spanish, say what type of weather you prefer.
10) Translate into English: 'Deme un cartón de zumo de naranja.'

Total:

Quiz 4 Date: ...... / ...... / ......

1) True or false? 'Un bote' means 'a boot'.
2) How do you say 'al final de la calle' in English?
3) In Spanish, give directions from your home to the nearest shop.
4) How do you say 'Habrá tormenta' in English?
5) What are these items of clothing in Spanish?
   a) socks   b) jacket   c) trainers   d) tie
6) Describe what the weather is currently like in Spanish.
7) What is 'un semáforo' in English?
8) Translate into English: '¿Hay otra talla?'
9) What is the Spanish for 'a portion'?
10) Give the English for: 'El servicio de reparto a domicilio es genial, pero quiero quejarme porque la rebeca está rasgada.'

Total:

Healthy and Unhealthy Living

Una vida sana

Para una vida saludable...	In order to lead ...
...intento .	...I try to drink lots of water.
...evito .	... junk food.
...como poca comida rápida.	...I eat .
...como .	... a balanced diet.
... al menos ocho horas cada noche.	...I sleep for each night.
Para mantenerme en forma, casi todos los días.	, I exercise .
mi salud mental...	I look after ...
...relajándome después del colegio...	... after school...
...y cada día.	...and going for a walk every day.

Una vida malsana

	(passive) smoker	*borracho/a*
	public places	*cigarette*
probar		*oler*
	soft / hard drug	*el sobrepeso*
emborracharse		*to get tired*

La gente que .... puede
.... el síndrome de abstinencia.
*People who stop smoking can
suffer* ....

Una vez, fui a .... ,
pero no me gustó.
.... *I went to a drinking party
in the street, but* ....

.... me preocupa
porque ....
Addiction to tobacco ....
because it's dangerous.

El humo .... los
pulmones y ....
.... *damages
and it smells awful.*

78

Second Go:
..... / ..... / .....

Healthy and Unhealthy Living

Una vida sana

	In order to lead a healthy life...
	...I try to drink lots of water.
	...I avoid junk food.
	...I eat little fast food.
	...I eat a balanced diet.
	...I sleep for at least eight hours each night.
	To keep fit, I exercise almost every day.
	I look after my mental health...
	...by relaxing after school...
	...and going for a walk every day.

Una vida malsana

	(passive) smoker		drunk
	public places		cigarette
	to try		to smell
	soft / hard drug		obesity
	to get drunk		to get tired

People who stop smoking can suffer withdrawal symptoms.

Once I went to a drinking party in the street, but I didn't like it.

Addiction to tobacco worries me because it's dangerous.

Smoke damages the lungs and it smells awful.

Topic 7 — Lifestyle

 ✓ ✓ ✓

Illnesses

Las enfermedades

....	to feel ill	seropositivo/a	....
encontrarse /			body
estar enfermo/a	....	....	heart
mejorarse		el hígado	
....	....	....	brain
....	pain	la depresión	....
el ataque cardíaco	....	la ansiedad	....
....	AIDS		

To say something hurts, use the verb '........' (to hurt). It works like 'gustar' — you need an indirect object pronoun before the verb and an 'n' in the plural.

.... la espalda.
.... hurts.

.... los pies.
.... hurt.

'doler' is a radical-changing verb.

Necesito ir al médico

................, me encontré mal y...	A month ago, ... and...
...tuve que	...I had to go to the doctor.
...el médico me dio	...the doctor .... a prescription.
Tengo dolor de estómago.	I have ....
De niño, tenía muchos	.... , I had a lot of respiratory problems.
Creo que .... un curso de primeros auxilios.	I think everyone should do ....
.... es un problema grave en algunos países.	The lack of doctors is .... in some countries.
Muchos jóvenes se preocupan por...	Lots of young people ....
... . y	...their weight and their appearance.
...sus exámenes, lo que	... . , which causes a lot of stress.

 ☑   ☑   ☑

Topic 7 — Lifestyle

Illnesses

Las enfermedades

....	to feel ill	....	HIV-positive
.... /		....	body
....	to be ill	....	heart
....	to get better	....	liver
....	pain	....	brain
....	heart attack	....	depression
....	AIDS	....	anxiety

To say ...., use the verb 'doler' (to hurt). It works like ' .... '
— you need .... before the verb and an ' ...... ' in the plural.

My back hurts.

My feet hurt.

'doler' is a
.... verb.

Necesito ir al médico

	A month ago, I was ill and... ...I had to go to the doctor. ...the doctor gave me a prescription.
	I have stomach ache.
	As a child, I had a lot of respiratory problems.
	I think everyone should do a first aid course.
	The lack of doctors is a serious problem in some countries.
	Lots of young people worry about... ...their weight and their appearance. ...their exams, which causes a lot of stress.

Mixed Practice Quizzes

You need to make sure you know your stuff about healthy living and illnesses.
These quizzes are a painless way to check how much you remember from p.77-80.

Quiz 1
Date: ...... / ...... / ......

1) Translate into English: 'Alguna gente se emborracha.'
2) 'Doing exercise helps to avoid obesity.' Say this in Spanish.
3) True or false? 'Doler' is a regular verb.
4) How do you say 'I eat little junk food' in Spanish?
5) What does 'mejorarse de una enfermedad' mean?
6) In Spanish, give one opinion on smoking.
7) How do you say 'seropositivo' in English?
8) Give the names of two organs from your body in Spanish.
9) Give the English for: 'El ejercicio mejora mi salud mental.'
10) 'Hace un mes, hice un curso de primeros auxilios.' Say this in English.

Total:

Quiz 2
Date: ...... / ...... / ......

1) How do you say 'Hard drugs are dangerous' in Spanish?
2) You go to the doctor because you have a sore throat and don't feel well. How would you tell them this in Spanish?
3) Give the Spanish for: 'I lead a healthy lifestyle.'
4) Translate into English: 'De niño, tenía muchos problemas de salud.'
5) What is 'un botellón'?
6) Translate into Spanish: 'The doctor gave my brother a prescription.'
7) How do you say 'anxiety' in Spanish?
8) Translate into English: 'Es importante comer una dieta equilibrada.'
9) In Spanish, give one thing that can worry young people.
10) What does 'cansarse fácilmente' mean in English?

Total:

Mixed Practice Quizzes

Quiz 3   Date: ...... / ...... / ......

1) How do you say 'sentirse mal' in English?

2) Answer this question in Spanish: '¿Cómo te mantienes en forma?'

3) What does 'oler fatal' mean in English?

4) Give the Spanish for: 'My arm hurts.'

5) True or false? 'La comida basura' means 'fast food' in English.

6) How do you say 'withdrawal symptoms' in Spanish?

7) What is 'depression' in Spanish?

8) 'Deberías dormir al menos ocho horas cada noche.'
Say this in English.

9) What is the English for 'el ataque cardíaco'?

10) Translate into Spanish: 'I will go to the doctor next week.'

Total:

Quiz 4   Date: ...... / ...... / ......

1) What is 'el tabaquismo'?

2) Give two ways to say 'to be ill' in Spanish.

3) 'I drink lots of water every day to stay healthy.' Say this in Spanish.

4) True or false? 'Enfermedad' is a masculine noun.

5) What is 'un dolor de espalda' in English?

6) What is the Spanish for 'You can't smoke in public places'?

7) How do you say 'el cuerpo' in English?

8) 'Intento relajarme después del colegio para cuidar de mi salud mental.'
Say this in English.

9) Translate into Spanish: 'AIDS is a serious problem in some countries.'

10) How do you say 'una vida malsana' in English?

Total:

Environmental Problems

El medio ambiente

	ozone layer	malgastar	
los productos químicos			wastage
	acid rain	la escasez	
dañar			flood
	to blame	la sequía	

	me preocupa.	Climate change	.
El uso de ciertos contamina el aire y causa .		The use of fuels and causes global warming.	
Debido al efecto invernadero, ...		Due to , temperatures rise...	
...lo que amenaza de algunos animales.		...which the survival of some animals.	
Los gases de escape son .		are very harmful.	

La deforestación

Los bosques son importantes porque .... la cantidad de dióxido de carbono en ....
.... *are important because they reduce the amount of* .... *in the atmosphere.*

Hoy en día cortamos muchos .... para producir combustibles o limpiar el terreno para .... Esto contribuye a la destrucción de .... , y al cambio climático.
.... *we cut down lots of trees* ....
or .... *for farming. This contributes to the destruction of forests, and* ....

Si no .... ahora, las selvas y los bosques ....
If we don't act now, the .... *and* .... *will disappear.*

Environmental Problems

El medio ambiente

	ozone layer		to waste
	chemicals		wastage
	acid rain		shortage
	to damage		flood
	to blame		drought

	Climate change worries me.
	The use of certain fuels pollutes the air and causes global warming.
	Due to the greenhouse effect, temperatures rise...
	...which threatens the survival of some animals.
	Exhaust fumes are very harmful.

La deforestación

Forests are important because they reduce the amount of carbon dioxide in the atmosphere.

Nowadays we cut down lots of trees to produce fuel or to clear land for farming. This contributes to the destruction of forests, and to climate change.

If we don't act now, the jungles and forests will disappear.

Environmental Problems

El desperdicio de agua

.... usar menos agua en nuestra ....
We must .... *in our daily lives.*

.... para todo el mundo. Sin agua, ... no
pueden sobrevivir. Es .... que no deberíamos agotar.
Water is necessary for .... *Without water, crops can't*
.... *It's an important resource that* ....

La contaminación y otros problemas graves

Las mareas negras .... el mar y las playas. ....
es nocivo para los pájaros y .... que viven en el mar.
.... *make the sea and the beaches dirty. Oil is*
harmful for .... *and the creatures that* ....

Es esencial que .... Sin ella, no sobreviviremos.
It's essential that we protect nature. Without it, ...

Es importante que .... los efectos del cambio
climático porque si no, ... en el futuro.
It's important that we combat the effects of ....
because if not, we're going to suffer in the future.

Quiero que para reducir la basura que .	I want us to do more to that we produce.
Es muy fácil reciclar cartón y .	It's very easy and plastic packaging.
Si seguimos produciendo ...	If so much rubbish...
...todos los vertederos estarán pronto.	...all will be full soon.
Es terrible que en las generaciones del futuro.	It's terrible that we don't think more about .

 ✓ ✓ ✓

Environmental Problems

El desperdicio de agua

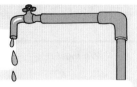

We must use less water in our daily lives.

Water is necessary for everyone. Without water, crops can't survive. It's an important resource that we shouldn't use up.

La contaminación y otros problemas graves

Oil spills make the sea and the beaches dirty. Oil is harmful for birds and the creatures that live in the sea.

It's essential that we protect nature. Without it, we won't survive.

It's important that we combat the effects of climate change because if not, we're going to suffer in the future.

	I want us to do more to reduce the rubbish that we produce.
	It's very easy to recycle cardboard and plastic packaging.
	If we continue producing so much rubbish... ...all the rubbish tips will be full soon.
	It's terrible that we don't think more about future generations.

Problems in Society

Los efectos de la guerra

...., muchas personas tienen que
emigrar a otro país y empezar la vida ....
Due to war, many people have .... *to*
another country and .... *all over again.*

> Use 'me parece' to say how something

...., hay .... y discriminación contra los
refugiados y .... que vienen a vivir a este país.
Unfortunately, there is prejudice and .... *against*
.... *and immigrants who come to live* ....

No me parece justo que .... que tienes
.... del país en que naciste.
.... *that the freedom you have*
depends so much on the country in which ....

La igualdad social

Sería creer que todos somos iguales, pero .	It'd be nice to believe that , but that's not the case.
La desigualdad crea entre y los pobres.	creates a gap between the rich and .
Me encantaría vivir en .	in a fairer society.

La violencia juvenil

En mi barrio, hay un grupo de .... que nos dan miedo.
.... *, there's a group of violent youths* ....

.... los grupos de gamberros que salen
por la noche e .... la gente mayor.
The groups of .... *who go out at night and*
intimidate .... *make me really angry.*

> '........................... ' changes to 'e' before words starting with 'i' or 'hi'.

Problems in Society

Los efectos de la guerra

Due to war, many people have to emigrate to
another country and start their lives all over again.

Use
....
to say how something
seems to you.

Unfortunately, there is prejudice and discrimination against
refugees and immigrants who come to live in this country.

It seems unfair to me that the freedom you have
depends so much on the country in which you were born.

La igualdad social

	It'd be nice to believe that we're all equal, but that's not the case.
	Inequality creates a gap between the rich and the poor.
	I would love to live in a fairer society.

La violencia juvenil

In my neighbourhood, there's a group of violent youths who scare us.

The groups of troublemakers who go out at night and
intimidate the older people make me really angry.

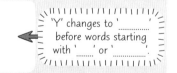

'Y' changes to '............'
before words starting
with '......' or '............'.

 ☑ ☑ ☑

Problems in Society

La pobreza

Creo que hay más pobreza que .	I think there's than ten years ago.
debería apoyar a los "sin techo".	The government should .
Vivo en , pero todavía hay mucha gente sin comida.	I live in a rich country, but there are still lots of people .
Deberíamos luchar para a porque...	to help the most needy people because...
...es fácil acabar sin hogar o en si pierdes tu trabajo.	...it's easy or in poverty if you lose your job.
La pobreza puede afectar a .	Poverty can anyone.

El desempleo

Mucha gente .... en mi ciudad.
Lots of people are unemployed in my city.

.... es un peligro, especialmente para los jóvenes.
.... dicen que son los más afectados.
Unemployment is ...., especially for young people.
The experts say they are ....

Si pudiera cambiar algo, ... porque el
desempleo es .... que debemos solucionar.
.... *change anything, I'd create more jobs because*
unemployment is a big problem that ....

Los que están en paro se encuentran en ....'
ya que es más difícil .... otro trabajo si estás en paro.
Those .... find themselves in a vicious circle,
as it's harder to find another job if ....

Topic 8 — Social and Global Issues

Problems in Society

La pobreza

	I think there's more poverty than ten years ago.
	The government should support homeless people.
	I live in a rich country, but there are still lots of people without food.
	We should fight to help the most needy people because... ...it's easy to end up homeless or in poverty if you lose your job.
	Poverty can affect anyone.

El desempleo

Lots of people are unemployed in my city.

Unemployment is a danger, especially for young people. The experts say they are the worst affected.

If I could change anything, I'd create more jobs because unemployment is a big problem that we must solve.

Those who are unemployed find themselves in a vicious circle, as it's harder to find another job if you're unemployed.

Topic 8 — Social and Global Issues

Contributing to Society

Ser ecológico/a

Participé en .... en contra del uso de los combustibles fósiles.
.... a protest against the use of ....

Deberíamos invertir en .... para ....
We should .... renewable energy to save the planet.

Para proteger	the environment...
...uso el transporte público.	...I use ....
... . por apagar las luces.	...I save energy by ....
...reutilizo .... en vez de comprar nuevas.	... . shopping bags instead of ....
... . siempre que puedo.	...I recycle rubbish whenever I can.

Ayudar a otros

Los domingos trabajo en .... y ayudo con el club de
jóvenes en mi pueblo. Es esencial que .... por los demás.
On Sundays I work in a charity shop and I help with ....
in my town. It's essential that we do something ....

.... es un problema que afecta mucho a los ancianos.
Todos deberíamos hacer más ....
Loneliness is an issue that .... a lot.
.... do more to look after them.

Acabo de lanzar .... para ....
de desastres naturales como .... e ....
.... a campaign to help the victims
of .... like hurricanes and fires.

Es importante que .... a las organizaciones benéficas.
It's important that we support ....

 ☑ ☑ ☑

Second Go:
..... / ..... / .....

Contributing to Society

Ser ecológico/a

I participated in a protest against the use of fossil fuels.

We should invest in renewable energy to save the planet.

	To protect the environment...
	...I use public transport.
	...I save energy by turning off the lights.
	...I reuse shopping bags instead of buying new ones.
	...I recycle rubbish whenever I can.

Ayudar a otros

On Sundays I work in a charity shop and I help with the youth club in my town. It's essential that we do something for others.

Loneliness is an issue that affects the elderly a lot.
We should all do more to look after them.

I have just launched a campaign to help the victims of natural disasters like hurricanes and fires.

It's important that we support charitable organisations.

Mixed Practice Quizzes

In the spirit of helping others and contributing to your Spanish knowledge, here are four more quizzes to help you check what you remember from p.83-92.

Quiz 1 | Date: ...... / ...... / ......

1) How do you say 'carbon dioxide' in Spanish?
2) Translate into English: 'El desempleo es un círculo vicioso.'
3) Translate into Spanish: 'I work with the elderly three times a week.'
4) What is 'perder la libertad' in English?
5) Give the Spanish for 'natural disasters like floods'.
6) 'We should recycle plastic packaging and cardboard.' Say this in Spanish.
7) In Spanish, give one reason why water shouldn't be wasted.
8) Give the English for 'los jóvenes violentos'.
9) What is 'Producimos muchos desechos plásticos' in English?
10) Translate into Spanish: 'I want us to think more about future generations.'

Total:

Quiz 2 | Date: ...... / ...... / ......

1) What is 'la escasez de recursos' in English?
2) True or false? 'Los gamberros' means 'youth workers' in English.
3) What does 'Los "sin techo" necesitan nuestra ayuda' mean in English?
4) Translate into Spanish: 'Oil spills are very harmful for birds.'
5) How do you say 'to launch a campaign' in Spanish?
6) Translate into English:
   'El gobierno debería apoyar a los que están en paro.'
7) What is the Spanish for 'They used to work in a charity shop'?
8) Give the English for: 'Quiero que reduzcamos la basura y reciclemos más.'
9) How do you say 'renewable fuels' in Spanish?
10) Give the Spanish for the following verbs:
    a) to waste   b) to damage   c) to blame

Total:

94

Mixed Practice Quizzes

Quiz 3   Date: ...... / ...... / ......

1) How do you say 'There is so much prejudice' in Spanish?
2) Give the English for: 'Es esencial que ayudemos a otras personas.'
3) What is 'the gap between the rich and the poor' in Spanish?
4) Give the English for: 'La pobreza afecta a demasiada gente.'
5) What is the Spanish for 'water wastage'?
6) Translate into English: 'Mis amigos trabajan con el club de jóvenes.'
7) How do you say 'The use of fossil fuels can cause acid rain' in Spanish?
8) True or false? 'El desempleo juvenil' is 'youth unemployment' in English.
9) 'Debemos actuar ahora para reducir el calentamiento global.'
   Translate this sentence into English.
10) 'People often have to emigrate to other countries.' Say this in Spanish.

Total:

Quiz 4   Date: ...... / ...... / ......

1) How do you say 'charitable organisation' in Spanish?
2) What is 'La naturaleza está en peligro' in English?
3) 'Deforestation contributes to climate change.' Say this in Spanish.
4) True or false? 'Perder un trabajo' means 'to lose a job' in English.
5) Translate into English: 'El agua es un recurso importante.'
6) Translate into Spanish: 'He wants to live in a more equal society.'
7) What is 'dañar la capa de ozono' in English?
8) 'Da un efecto de la pobreza.' Give your answer in Spanish.
9) Translate into English: 'Los refugiados sufren discriminación.'
10) Give the Spanish for: 'Loneliness can affect anyone.'

Total:

Topic 8 — Social and Global Issues

Where to Go

First Go:
..... /..... /.....

Los países y las nacionalidades

England

Escocia

Wales

Northern Ireland

Gran Bretaña

Alemania

Italy

Europe

Mi padre es ....,
así que vamos a .... a menudo.
.... _is half Irish, so_
.... _to Ireland._

.... y la mayoría de
mi familia vive en ....
I'm Greek and ....
my family live in Greece.

Hace dos años, ... a ....
y a Colombia con mis amigas ....
.... , _I went to the United States_
and Colombia with my Scottish ....

.... le encanta viajar.   .... a Argentina, Perú y Chile.
También le interesan .... y la comida mexicana.
My sister .... _She's travelled to Argentina, Peru and_
Chile. .... _in Brazilian culture and Mexican food._

¿Adónde quisiera ir de vacaciones?

Este verano, ... al norte de .... y a Portugal.	This .... , I hope to go to the .... of France and Portugal.
Me encantaría	.... to visit Cuba...
...porque las playas son	...because the .... are beautiful.
.... es el destino de mis sueños...	Australia is my ....
...porque .... la Gran Barrera de Coral.	...because I want to see the ....
Quiero ir a .... para esquiar.	I want to go to Canada ....
.... ir a	I dream of going to India...
...para ver elefantes salvajes.	...to see ....

Where to Go

Los países y las nacionalidades

England

Scotland

Wales

Northern Ireland

Great Britain

Germany

Italy

Europe

My father is half Irish, so
we often go to Ireland.

I'm Greek and most of my
family live in Greece.

Two years ago, I went to the United States
and Colombia with my Scottish friends.

My sister loves travelling. She's travelled to Argentina, Peru and
Chile. She's also interested in Brazilian culture and Mexican food.

¿Adónde quisiera ir de vacaciones?

	This summer, I hope to go to the north of France and Portugal.
	I'd love to visit Cuba... ...because the beaches are beautiful.
	Australia is my dream destination... ...because I want to see the Great Barrier Reef.
	I want to go to Canada to ski.
	I dream of going to India... ...to see wild elephants.

Accommodation

El alojamiento

....	*state-owned hotel*	un hotel de lujo	....
las instalaciones	....	(irse de) camping	....
....	*double room*		*tent*
la habitación individual	....	....	*cruise*

Quisiera alojarme en...

.... alojarme cuatro noches en	I would like .... for four nights in a boarding house.
Necesitamos una habitación...	.... a room...
... . aire acondicionado.	...that has ....
...que tenga	...that has a bathroom.
.... una habitación...	I would prefer a room...
...con vista al mar.	...with ....
...con balcón.	...with ....
...con	...with a double bed.
Me quedo en	I stay in a youth hostel...
...para .... gente nueva.	...in order to meet ....
...para ahorrar dinero.	...in order to ....
Preferirían alojarse en un camping...	They'd prefer to stay on a ....
...porque tienen	...because they have a caravan...
...y les gusta la naturaleza.	...and they like ....
Mi amigo quisiera .... alojamiento de media pensión.	My friend would like to find ....
Preferiría reservar	I'd prefer to book full-board accommodation.
Por favor, ¿puedo reservar .... habitación disponible?	Please can I reserve the best room .... ?

98

Accommodation

El alojamiento

....	state-owned hotel	....	luxury hotel
....	facilities	....	(to go) camping
....	double room	....	tent
....	single room	....	cruise

Quisiera alojarme en...

	I would like to stay for four nights in a boarding house.
	We need a room... ...that has air-conditioning. ...that has a bathroom.
	I would prefer a room... ...with a sea view. ...with a balcony. ...with a double bed.
	I stay in a youth hostel... ...in order to meet new people. ...in order to save money.
	They'd prefer to stay on a campsite... ...because they have a caravan... ...and they like nature.
	My friend would like to find half-board accommodation.
	I'd prefer to book full-board accommodation.
	Please can I reserve the best room available?

Getting Ready and Getting There

Las preparaciones

.... del alojamiento disponible en ....
I found out about the .... accommodation at the travel agent's.

Ya he hecho mi ...., pero todavía no he comprado ....
Necesito una que .... información sobre Suiza e ....
I've .... packed my suitcase but I haven't bought a guidebook ....
.... *that includes information about* .... *and Italy.*

El guía nos dió .... mientras nos mostraba ....
.... *gave us some leaflets* .... *showing us the exhibits.*

Cómo llegar a tu destino

.... a España fue largo... ...porque .... en coche.	The journey to Spain was ....because we went by ....
Tuvimos que .... en muchas estaciones de servicio para llenar el tanque con	We had to stop at lots of .... to .... with petrol.
.... en barcos... ...así que preferiría ir en avión.	I feel travel sick on ....so I'd prefer ....
Compré .... para ir a Toledo desde Madrid.	.... a return ticket to go to Toledo .... Madrid.
.... la ciudad a pie y fui en taxi	I explored the city .... and I went by taxi to the castle.
.... en el Casco Histórico.	I got lost in the ....
No me importa viajar en .... pero prefiero el ferrocarril.	.... travelling by coach but I prefer ....
.... en Valencia te permite ver .... la ciudad.	The tram in Valencia .... see a lot of the city.

Getting Ready and Getting There

Las preparaciones

I found out about the available accommodation at the travel agent's.

I've already packed my suitcase but I haven't bought a guidebook yet.
I need one that includes information about Switzerland and Italy.

The guide gave us some leaflets while showing us the exhibits.

Cómo llegar a tu destino

	The journey to Spain was long... ...because we went by car.
	We had to stop at lots of service stations to fill the tank with petrol.
	I feel travel sick on boats... ...so I'd prefer to go by plane.
	I bought a return ticket to go to Toledo from Madrid.
	I explored the city on foot and I went by taxi to the castle.
	I got lost in the Old Town.
	I don't mind travelling by coach but I prefer the railway.
	The tram in Valencia lets you see a lot of the city.

Getting There and What to Do

Los problemas al viajar

.... deben hacer transbordo en la
.... porque este tren ha sido cancelado.
Passengers must .... *at the next station*
because this train ....

Coge el metro .... hay un atasco en ....
Take the .... *as there's a* .... *on the motorway.*

.... será en autobús porque los
empleados del aeropuerto ....
The return will be .... *because the*
.... *are on strike.*

El tren en ....
está retrasado ....
The train on this platform
.... *by an hour.*

Perdí mi pasaporte .... vuelo, así que .... alquilar un coche.
Tuve que .... y mostrar mi carnet de conducir.
I lost my .... *before the flight, so I had to* ....
I had to fill out a form and show my ....

¿Qué hiciste durante tus vacaciones?

la excursión			to take photos
el recuerdo		broncearse	
	to walk		theme park
	to ski	el parque de atracciones	

Pasamos cada día ...	every day on the beach...
...porque .	...because it was sunny.
Me bañé en el mar...	in the sea...
...y con mis primos.	...and sunbathed with my .
Me gusta nada más que nueva comida.	I like trying new food.
También pasé mucho tiempo haciendo .	I also spent doing water sports.

Getting There and What to Do

Los problemas al viajar

> Passengers must change at the next station
> because this train has been cancelled.

> Take the underground as there's a traffic jam on the motorway.

> The return will be by bus because the
> airport workers are on strike.

> The train on this platform
> is delayed by an hour.

> I lost my passport before the flight, so I had to hire a
> car. I had to fill out a form and show my driving licence.

¿Qué hiciste durante tus vacaciones?

	trip, excursion		to take photos
	souvenir		to get a tan
	to walk		theme park
	to ski		fairground

	We spent every day on the beach... ...because it was sunny.
	I swam in the sea... ...and sunbathed with my cousins.
	I like nothing more than trying new food.
	I also spent a lot of time doing water sports.

 ☑ ☑ ☑

Mixed Practice Quizzes

It's time for a quiz break. Yay! Test what you've learnt on p.95-102 with these quick questions. Don't forget to check your answers and add up your scores.

Quiz 1
Date: ...... / ...... / ......

1) How would you say you would like to reserve a room with a sea view in Spanish?

2) Translate into English: 'La mayoría de mi familia vive en Irlanda del Norte.'

3) Translate into Spanish: 'I got lost in Madrid.'

4) True or false? 'Tomar el sol' means 'to get a tan'.

5) In Spanish, say that you hope to go to Mexico this summer.

6) Give the English for: 'Debéis hacer transbordo en la próxima estación.'

7) If you were in 'la agencia de viajes', where would you be?

8) Translate into Spanish: 'We had to hire a car.'

9) Your friend says: 'Se quedan en un hotel de lujo.' What does this mean?

10) How would you say you've travelled to France and the USA in Spanish?

Total:

Quiz 2
Date: ...... / ...... / ......

1) Give the English for: 'Pasé cada día en el parque temático.'

2) Marco needs a single room with a balcony. Say this in Spanish.

3) Translate into Spanish: 'They dream of going to Australia with their friends.'

4) What does 'alojamiento de pensión completa' mean?

5) In Spanish, how would you tell someone that your sister feels travel sick on planes, so she prefers to travel by car?

6) Diego says: 'Todos los vuelos han sido cancelados.' What does this mean?

7) True or false? 'Service station' is 'la estación de servicio' in Spanish.

8) How would you say that Peru is your dream destination in Spanish?

9) Translate into English: 'Necesitas hacer tu maleta.'

10) Say that your friends would like to go camping in Spanish.

Total:

Mixed Practice Quizzes

Quiz 3 — Date: ...... / ...... / ......

1) In Spanish, say that you've stayed in lots of state-owned hotels.
2) Galia will go to Italy in winter to ski. How do you say this in Spanish?
3) Give the Spanish for: 'The underground workers were on strike.'
4) Your penfriend tells you: 'Me encantaría visitar India porque las playas son hermosas.' What are they saying?
5) Translate into Spanish: 'I like nothing more than swimming in the sea.'
6) True or false? 'El guía' means 'guidebook' in English.
7) In Spanish, how would you say that your grandmother is half Scottish?
8) Give the Spanish for: 'I stay on a campsite in order to meet new people.'
9) 'Siempre reservo la mejor habitación disponible.' What does this mean?
10) Translate into English: 'El viaje fue muy largo porque viajamos en autocar.'

Total:

Quiz 4 — Date: ...... / ...... / ......

1) In Spanish, tell your friend that you have some leaflets about Switzerland.
2) Translate into Spanish: 'I would like to stay for a week in a caravan.'
3) 'Fuiste varias veces al parque de atracciones.' What does this mean?
4) How would you say that you often used to go to Wales in Spanish?
5) Give the English for: 'Es mejor explorar una ciudad a pie.'
6) Translate into English: 'Siempre nos ha interesado la cultura griega.'
7) In Spanish, say your brother lost his passport before the flight.
8) You buy 'un billete de ida y vuelta' at the station. What is this?
9) 'Two years ago, I stayed at a youth hostel. There weren't many facilities and my room didn't have a bathroom.' Say this in Spanish.
10) Give the English for: 'Cogerá el tren porque hay un atasco en la autopista.'

Total:

School Subjects and School Supplies

First Go: ..... / ..... / .....

Las asignaturas

el alemán

Spanish

las matemáticas

drama

el inglés

French

las ciencias económicas

business studies

food technology

science

la biología

la física

los trabajos manuales

gymnastics

RE

la educación física

son...	My favourite subjects are...
...el dibujo y la informática...	... and ...
...porque se puede .	...because you can be creative.
Me encanta la historia...	...
...porque es interesante y útil .	...because and useful to learn about the past.
Nos gusta la química...	...
...ya que ver reacciones químicas.	...as it's fascinating to see .
Miguel odia ...	Miguel geography...
...porque aburrida.	...because he finds it .

En mi mochila

la agenda

exercise book

timetable

This is often shortened to 'el boli'. ➡ el bolígrafo

el libro

las tijeras

En mi mochila, hay .	In my , there's a pencil case.
Se me ha olvidado .	my pencil.
¿Me puedes prestar ?	Can you me a ruler?

   Topic 10 — Current and Future Study and Employment

School Subjects and School Supplies

Las asignaturas

Spanish	maths
German	drama
French	economics
English	business studies
science	food technology
biology	handicrafts
physics	gymnastics
RE	PE

	My favourite subjects are... ...art and IT... ...because you can be creative.
	I love history... ...because it's interesting and useful to learn about the past.
	We like chemistry... ...as it's fascinating to see chemical reactions.
	Miguel hates geography... ...because he finds it boring.

En mi mochila

diary	*This is often shortened to*
timetable	
book	

exercise book	
pen	
scissors	

	In my school bag, there's a pencil case.
	I have forgotten my pencil.
	Can you lend me a ruler?

Topic 10 — Current and Future Study and Employment

School Routine

Mi rutina escolar

_____ empieza a las nueve.	My school starts at _____ .
Vamos al salón de actos y el profesor _____ .	We go to _____ and the teacher calls the register.
Tengo _____ y cada clase dura cuarenta minutos.	I have five lessons a day and each lesson _____ .
Durante _____ ...	During break...
...juego al fútbol en el campo.	...I play football _____ .
... _____ con mis amigos.	...I chat with my friends.
...prefiero ir a la biblioteca.	...I prefer to go _____ .
_____ ...	At lunchtime...
...almorzamos en _____ .	... _____ in the canteen.
... _____ juntos afuera.	...we sit _____ together.
_____ termina a las cuatro.	The school day _____ .
Vuelvo a casa a _____ .	_____ at ten past four.
Hay _____ de cuatro meses en _____ .	There are three terms in the school year.

Las reglas

Hay que .... antes de hablar.
You have to raise your hand ....

Tienes que .... al menos tres veces a la semana.
You have to do sport at least ....

No deberías ni .... ni beber bebidas gaseosas.
.... *eat chewing gum or* ....

Es obligatorio llevar ....
y .... llevar maquillaje.
.... *to wear a uniform and you can't* ....

    Topic 10 — Current and Future Study and Employment

108

School Routine

Mi rutina escolar

	My school starts at nine o'clock.
	We go to the assembly room and the teacher calls the register.
	I have five lessons a day and each lesson lasts forty minutes.
	During break... ...I play football on the field. ...I chat with my friends. ...I prefer to go to the library.
	At lunchtime... ...we eat lunch in the canteen. ...we sit outside together.
	The school day finishes at four.
	I return home at ten past four.
	There are three four-month-long terms in the school year.

Las reglas

You have to raise your hand before speaking.

You have to do sport at least three times a week.

You shouldn't eat chewing gum or drink fizzy drinks.

It's compulsory to wear a uniform and you can't wear make-up.

Topic 10 — Current and Future Study and Employment

School Life and School Pressures

¿Cómo es tu colegio?

primary school   el taller

la sala de profesores   classroom

el gimnasio   religioso/a

changing rooms   private

Me llevo bien con .	with the teachers.
Hay tales como las pizarras interactivas.	There are modern facilities such as .
Es un instituto mixto y público con .	It's with six hundred students.

El estrés y la vida escolar

stressful   repasar

el éxito   bullying

to pass   el apoyo

suspender   to support

Tengo .	I have too much homework.
Hay mucha presión para .	There's to get good marks.
Necesito para ir a la universidad.	I need to get outstanding marks in order
El mal comportamiento las clases ya que es una distracción.	ruins lessons as it is .
tienen una falta de respeto hacia .	Some students have for others.
En mi colegio es un problema muy ...	bullying is a serious problem...
...y ocurren a menudo.	...and fights often.

School Life and School Pressures

¿Cómo es tu colegio?

	primary school		workshop
	staffroom		classroom
	gymnasium		religious
	changing rooms		private

	I get on well with the teachers.
	There are modern facilities such as smart boards.
	It's a mixed state school with six hundred students.

El estrés y la vida escolar

	stressful		to revise
	success		bullying
	to pass		support
	to fail		to support

	I have too much homework.
	There's a lot of pressure to get good marks.
	I need to get outstanding marks in order to go to university.
	Bad behaviour ruins lessons as it is a distraction.
	Some students have a lack of respect for others.
	In my school bullying is a serious problem...
	...and fights happen often.

Education Post-16

Cuando tenga 16 años...

Quiero _____ y hacer el bachillerato.
I want to continue my studies and _____.

Tengo la intención de ir a _____ para estudiar música.
_____ *to go to an academy* _____.

Nuestra profesora _____ que busquemos experiencia laboral.
Our teacher recommends that we look for _____.

Hacer una práctica mejorará _____.
Doing _____ *will improve my work prospects.*

_____, pero espero hacerme aprendiza de fontanero.
It'll be challenging, but I hope to become _____.

Después del bachillerato...

Voy a ____ a mis estudios...	I'm going to focus on ...
...porque quiero conseguir ____.	...because I want ____ a degree.
...porque ____ traductor.	...because I want to be ____.
Quisiera tomarme ____ antes de ir a la universidad.	I would like to take a gap year ____.
Quiero ser electricista, así que necesitaré ____.	I want to be ____, so I will need professional training.
____ ir a la universidad si quieres ____ en medicina.	You must go to university if you want to have a career ____.
Haré un aprendizaje para ____.	I will do ____ to become a qualified carpenter.

Education Post-16

Cuando tenga 16 años...

I want to continue my studies and do my A-levels.

I intend to go to an academy to study music.

Our teacher recommends that we look for work experience.

Doing a work placement will improve my work prospects.

It'll be challenging, but I hope to become a plumber's apprentice.

Después del bachillerato...

	I'm going to focus on my studies... ...because I want to get a degree. ...because I want to be a translator.
	I would like to take a gap year before going to university.
	I want to be an electrician, so I will need professional training.
	You must go to university if you want to have a career in medicine.
	I will do an apprenticeship to become a qualified carpenter.

Career Choices and Ambitions

Los empleos

| | lawyer | | firefighter |

nurse   carpintero/a

veterinario/a   comerciante

jefe/a   police officer

cocinero/a   camionero/a

builder   painter

	sería periodista, trabajando en .	My ideal job would be , working in an office.
Adjunto para solicitar el puesto de .	I attach my CV the of accountant.
Tengo un año de experiencia.	I have .
Tengo para el puesto de ingeniero.	I have an interview for .
, un trabajo debe ser... ... y gratificante.	For me, should be... ...stimulating and .

Un empleo a tiempo parcial

Tengo un empleo .... así que .... paga.
I have a part-time job so I don't get ....

.... es que hay descuentos para ....
The best thing is that .... for employees.

Trabajo en .... los sábados. Me gusta .... con los clientes.
I work in a hairdresser's .... I like chatting with ....

Soy un camarero trabajador. Me gusta mi trabajo, pero ....
I'm .... I like .... , but I don't earn a lot.

Espero conseguir .... que tenga un buen sueldo.
.... to find a varied job that has ....

 ☑   ☑   ☑   Topic 10 — Current and Future Study and Employment

Career Choices and Ambitions

Los empleos

	lawyer		firefighter
	nurse		carpenter
	vet		shop owner
	boss		police officer
	chef		lorry driver
	builder		painter

	My ideal job would be a journalist, working in an office.
	I attach my CV to apply for the position of accountant.
	I have a year's experience.
	I have an interview for the position of engineer.
	For me, a job should be... ...stimulating and rewarding.

Un empleo a tiempo parcial

I have a part-time job so I don't get pocket money.

The best thing is that there are discounts for employees.

I work in a hairdresser's on Saturdays. I like chatting with customers.

I'm a hard-working waiter. I like my job, but I don't earn a lot.

I hope to find a varied job that has a good salary.

Mixed Practice Quizzes

Before you leave the topic of school behind, let's see how much vocab from p.105-114 has sunk in. Have a go at all the quizzes, then tot up your scores.

Quiz 1 Date: ...... / ...... / ......

1) Translate into English: 'Hay mucha presión para aprobar los exámenes.'

2) '¿Me puedes prestar unas tijeras?' How do you say this in English?

3) Give the Spanish for: 'I would like to apply for the position of nurse.'

4) 'Es obligatorio levantar la mano antes de hablar.' What does this mean?

5) In Spanish, say your friend doesn't like her part-time job because it isn't very stimulating.

6) Give the English for: 'Quisiera hacer una práctica en una oficina.'

7) Say 'We want to focus on our studies and do our A-levels' in Spanish.

8) How would you say your favourite subject is business studies in Spanish?

9) Gerardo goes to 'un instituto privado'. What does this mean?

10) Translate into English: 'Durante el recreo, prefieren sentarse afuera.'

Total:

Quiz 2 Date: ...... / ...... / ......

1) In Spanish, say that you intend to do an apprenticeship after your A-Levels.

2) Give the English for: 'Los profesores dan mucho apoyo a los alumnos.'

3) 'My ideal job would be a vet because it's rewarding.' Say this in Spanish.

4) Translate into English: 'Él odia la historia, pero yo la encuentro fascinante.'

5) True or false? 'El salón de actos' means 'workshop' in English.

6) Translate into Spanish: 'We hope to find another job as we don't earn a lot.'

7) Nial says: 'Unas aulas tienen pizarras interactivas.' What does this mean?

8) How would you say that you want to go to an academy in Spanish?

9) Give the Spanish for: 'Everyone has to do sport at least twice a week.'

10) 'Se le ha olvidado su cuaderno para matemáticas.' What does this mean in English?

Total:

Mixed Practice Quizzes

Quiz 3

Date: ...... / ...... / ......

1) Translate into English: 'El mal comportamiento es un problema grave.'

2) How would you ask someone if they can lend you a pen in Spanish?

3) Your teacher says: 'Recomiendo que sigáis vuestros estudios.'
   What does this mean in English?

4) How do you say 'Adjunto mi currículum' in English?

5) Give the Spanish for: 'They don't get on well with their teachers.'

6) '¿Vas a tomarte un año sabático?' How do you say this in English?

7) Translate into English: 'Les gustan mucho los trabajos manuales.'

8) How do you say that your school starts at eight thirty in Spanish?

9) Give the English for: 'Creo que ser bombero sería muy desafiante.'

10) Tell your friend you don't have to wear a uniform in Spanish.

Total:

Quiz 4

Date: ...... / ...... / ......

1) In Spanish, say that there's a pencil case and a diary in your school bag.

2) What are 'las perspectivas laborales' in English?

3) Translate into English: 'Busca un trabajo a tiempo parcial que sea variado.'

4) Give two words which mean 'bullying' in Spanish.

5) What does 'Las clases duran cincuenta minutos' mean in English?

6) Say in Spanish: 'He loves food technology because he can be creative.'

7) Give the Spanish for: 'Some students ruin lessons
   regularly, but fights don't happen often.'

8) 'Se necesitará formación profesional para hacerse electricista calificado.'
   What does this mean in English?

9) Give the English for: 'Mis amigos y yo almorzamos juntos en la cantina.'

10) How would you say that you would like to be a lawyer
    because they receive a good salary in Spanish?

Total:

Topic 10 — Current and Future Study and Employment

Words for People and Objects

Gender of nouns

Masculine nouns have 'el' or '⬚' before them and are usually:

Nouns that end in: -o, -l, -n, -r, -s, -ta, -aje	Male people, days, ⬚, languages, seas, ⬚, oceans and mountains.

..... árbol *tree*   ..... atún *tuna*   ..... francés *French*

Feminine nouns have 'la' or '⬚' before them and are usually:

Nouns that end in: -a, -ción, -sión, -tad, -tud, -dad, -umbre	⬚, letters of the alphabet.

..... casa *house*   ..... canción *song*   ..... edad *age*

You can't tell the gender of a noun ending in '⬚' or '⬚'. You just have to learn them:

⬚ *the car*   ⬚ *the tourist (male)*

⬚ *the people*   ⬚ *the tourist (female)*

Common exceptions:

el día   ⬚   *map*   ⬚   *motorbike*

⬚ *problem*   *photo*   la mano

Making nouns plural

To make most nouns that end in
a vowel plural, just add '⬚'.   una cama ⮕ dos ....
Exceptions:

① For nouns ending in consonants (not 'z'), add '⬚'.   una flor ⮕ dos ....

② For nouns ending in 'z', drop the 'z' and add '⬚'.   un lápiz ⮕ dos ....

③ For days ending in '⬚' and
⬚, only change the article.   el viernes ⮕ los ....   los Taylor

You may need to add or remove an ⬚ from   un inglés ⮕ dos ....
some plurals to keep the ⬚ the same.

118

Words for People and Objects

Gender of nouns

Masculine nouns have '   ' or '   ' before them and are usually:

Nouns that end in: , -l, -n, , -s, -ta,	Male people, , months, , seas, rivers, and .

tree   *tuna*   *French*

Feminine nouns have '   ' or '   ' before them and are usually:

Nouns that end in: , -ción, , -tad, -tud, , -umbre	Female people, of the

house   *song*   *age*

You   the gender of a noun ending in '   ' or '   '.
You just have to learn them:

     the car   *the tourist (male)*
     the people   *the tourist (female)*

Common   :

     day   *map*   *motorbike*
     problem   *photo*   *hand*

Making nouns plural

To make most nouns that end in   plural, just   .   *una cama* ➡

Exceptions:

1 For nouns ending in   (not '   '), add '   '.   *una flor* ➡

2 For nouns ending in 'z',   and add '   '.   *un lápiz* ➡

3 For   ending in '   ' and surnames, only change   .   *el viernes* ➡   *los Taylor*

You may need to   or   an   from some plurals to keep the   the same.   *un inglés* ➡

'The', 'A', 'Some' and Other Little Words

_____ articles

_____ articles are for specific things — the dog(s), the door(s).

_____ perro   _____ perros   _____ puerta   _____ puertas

' _____ ' is also used for feminine nouns that start with a _____ 'a', e.g. ' _____ agua'.

You _____ a definite article in Spanish when you wouldn't in English:

1 nouns used in a _____ sense   Me gusta ____ café. I like _____ .

2 days of the week and _____   _____ lunes a _____ seis Mondays at six o'clock

3 weights and _____   dos euros _____ kilo two euros a kilo

4 with a person's _____   ¿Cómo está ____ señor Tan? _____ Mr Tan?

Use ' ___ ' for things that aren't masculine or feminine.
Any adjective that follows it should be _____ .

_____ peor es que...
The _____ thing is that...

_____ articles

_____ articles refer to general things, e.g. a dog, some doors.

_____ perro   _____ perros   _____ puerta   _____ puertas

_____ articles are left out after a _____ verb, and after 'ser' when talking about someone's _____ or _____ .

Soy _____ . I'm a student.   _____ perro. I haven't got _____ .

Any, other, each, all

There's no special word for ' ___ ' in Spanish.   ¿Tienes uvas? Have you got _____ ?

Use ' _____ ' for 'another'. You don't need ' ___ ' or ' ___ ' before it.   Lo haré _____ día. I'll _____ another day.

'Cada' means ' ___ '. It's the same for _____ and _____ nouns.   Cada _____ voy a Gales.
_____ autumn I go to _____ .

'Todo/a/os/as' means ' ___ '.   Compré todas las _____ . I bought ____ the chairs.

Second Go: ..... / ..... / ..... 'The', 'A', 'Some' and Other Little Words

Definite articles

Definite articles are for [____] things — the dog(s), the door(s).

[....... perro] [........... perros] [....... puerta] [........... puertas]

You may need a definite article in Spanish when you [_____] :

'...........' is also used for .... nouns that start with a .... 'a', e.g. '........ agua'.

1 nouns used in a [_____] — *I like coffee.*

2 [____] of the [____] and [____] — *Mondays at six o'clock*

3 [____] and [____] — *two euros a kilo*

4 with a [_____] — *How is Mr Tan?*

Use '[__]' for things that aren't [_____] or [____] .
Any [_____] that follows it should be [_____] . — *The worst thing is that...*

Indefinite articles

Indefinite articles refer to [____] things, e.g. a dog, some doors.

[....... perro] [............. perros] [............. puerta] [............... puertas]

Indefinite articles are [____] after a [____] verb, and after '[__]' when talking about someone's [____] or [____] .

I'm a student. — *I haven't got a dog.*

Any, each, other, all

There's [_____] for 'any' in Spanish. — *Have you got any grapes?*

Use '[____]' for 'another'. You don't need '[__]' or '[__]' before it. — *I'll do it another day.*

'[____]' means 'each'. It's the same for [_____] . — *Each autumn I go to Wales.*

'[_____]' means 'all'. — *I bought all the chairs.*

Topic 11 — Grammar

Words to Describe Things

Agreement

el chico baj.....   la chica baj.....   los chicos baj.......   las chicas baj.......

Adjectives that don't end in '   ' don't change in the [   ]. In the plural, add 's' if the adjective ends in a [   ], or 'es' if it ends in a [   ].

la mujer trist.....
las mujeres trist.......

Some adjectives don't [   ] to agree. Most of these are [   ].

lila   beige   [   ]   orange   [   ]   rosa

tres coches ....
three orange ....

Position and [   ]

Most adjectives go [   ] the noun, but some always go [   ] it:

mucho/a   [   ]   little   primero/a, segundo/a...   [   ]   ...
muchos/as   [   ]   pocos/as   [   ]   next
[   ]   another   [   ]   so much   last
[   ]   other   tantos/as   [   ]
alguno/a   [   ]   each

'Bueno/a', 'primero/a', 'tercero/a', 'alguno/a', 'ninguno/a' and 'malo/a' all [   ] the [   ] in front of a singular noun. 'Alguno/a' and 'ninguno/a' also gain an [   ] on the '   '.

un ....
a good day

Position can change the [   ] of some adjectives:

'Grande' is the only adjective that drops '.....' in front of both .... and .... nouns.

Before the noun...	After the noun...
un gran hombre — *a [ ] man*	un hombre grande — *a [ ] man*
el [ ] día — *the same day*	yo [ ] — *I myself*
un [ ] coche — *a new (to owner) car*	un coche [ ] — *a brand new car*
un viejo amigo — *a [ ] friend*	un amigo viejo — *an [ ] friend*

Second Go:
..... / ..... / .....

Words to Describe Things

Agreement

| el chico bajo | la chica .... | los chicos .... | las chicas .... |

Adjectives that don't [____] don't change in [____]. In the plural, add ' [__] ' if the adjective ➔ la mujer triste
ends in a vowel, or ' [__] ' if it ends in a consonant.   las ....

Some adjectives don't [____] . Most of these are [____] .

[__] beige   [__] orange
[__] lilac   [__] pink   three orange cars

Position and meaning

Most adjectives go [____] , but [____] always go [____] :

[____]	a lot of	[____]	little	[____]	first,
	lots of		few		... second...
	another		so much		next
	other		so many		last
	some		each		

' [____] ' 'primero/a', ' [____] ', 'alguno/a', ' [____] ' and
' [____] ' all lose the [____] in front of a [____] .
noun. 'Alguno/a' and 'ninguno/a' also gain [____] .   a good day

[____] can change the [____]
of some adjectives:

╱⎺⎺⎺⎺⎺⎺⎺⎺⎺⎺⎺⎺⎺⎺⎺⎺⎺⎺⎺⎺⎺⎺⎺⎺⎺⎺╲
' .... ' is the only adjective that drops ' .... '
in front of both .... and ....
╲_____╱

Before the noun...	After the noun...
[____] — a great man	[____] — a big man
[____] — the same day	[____] — I myself
[____] — a new (to owner) car	[____] — a brand new car
a long-standing friend	an old (elderly) friend

      ☑   ☑ ☺ ☑

Words to Describe Things

Possessive adjectives

These need to [____] with the [____] they're describing — not the person or thing that [____] it.

tu gato | tus gat____

There are short and long forms of possessive adjectives. The short forms go [____] the [____], but the long forms (in brackets) go [____].

mi libro | el libro ____

Possessive	Masc. sing.	Fem. sing.	Masc. pl.	Fem. pl.
my	mi (mío)	mi (mía)		
your (inf. sing.)		tu (tuya)	tus (tuyos)	
his / her / its / your (form. sing.)	su (suyo)		sus (suyos)	
our				nuestras
your (inf. pl.)		vuestra	vuestros	
their / your (form. pl.)				sus (suyas)

Other adjectives

[____] adjectives are 'this', '[____]', 'that', '[____]', 'that over there', and 'those over there'. They need to [____] with the [____] they describe.

[____] *this* | [____] *that* | [____] *that over there*
estos/as | esos/as | [____] *those over there*

____ tigre
this tiger

esas faldas
....

_____
that car over there

____ leche
that ____ over there

'Cuyo' is a [____] adjective and means '[____]'. It shows who something belongs to and agrees with the [____] it is describing (not with the [____]).

_____ cuyo gato está allí.
She is the girl ____ cat ____.

Es el hombre _____.
He _____ whose daughters I know.

Topic 11 — Grammar

124

Words to Describe Things

Possessive adjectives

These need to ⬚ with the ⬚ — not the person or thing that ⬚.

tu gato | tus ....

There are ⬚ and ⬚ forms of possessive adjectives. The ⬚ forms go before the noun, but the ⬚ forms (in brackets) go ⬚.

mi libro | el libro ....

Possessive	Masc. sing.	Fem. sing.	Masc. pl.	Fem. pl.
my				
your (inf. sing.)				
his / her / its / your (form. sing.)				
our				
your (inf. pl.)				
their / your (form. pl.)				

Other adjectives

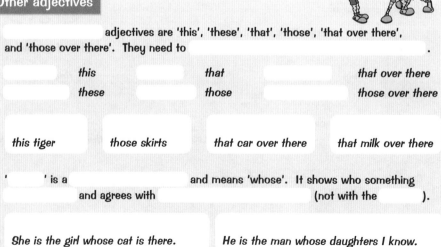

⬚ adjectives are 'this', 'these', 'that', 'those', 'that over there', and 'those over there'. They need to ⬚.

⬚ this ⬚ that ⬚ that over there
these those those over there

this tiger | those skirts | that car over there | that milk over there

' ⬚ ' is a ⬚ and means 'whose'. It shows who something ⬚ and agrees with ⬚ (not with the ⬚).

She is the girl whose cat is there. | He is the man whose daughters I know.

 ☑ ☑ ☑

Words to Compare Things

Comparatives and superlatives

| más ... (que ...) | ... (...) | El piso es más barato que la casa.
 The flat is .... than the house. |

| ... the most ... | El piso es .... barato.
 The flat is the cheapest. |

| menos... (que...) | ... (...) | El piso es menos barato que la casa.
 The flat is .... cheap .... the house. |

| ... the least ... | El piso es .... barato.
 The flat is the least cheap. |

| tan ... como ... | ... ... | El piso es tan barato como la casa.
 The flat is .... the house. |

The 'el' in   and   has to   with what it describes.

Laura es la más baja.
 Laura is ....

Jo y Ed son .... altos.
 Jo and Ed are the least ....

CHEAP!

Exceptions

You don't use '   ' or '   ' with these comparative and superlative forms:

Adjective	Comparative	Superlative
bueno (good)	(better)	(the best)
(bad)	(worse)	el peor (the worst)
viejo (old)	(older)	(the oldest)
joven ( )	( )	el menor ( )

If the noun is feminine or   , the superlative '   ' changes to agree. In the   , you also need to add '   ' to the adjective.

Lia y Aina son ....
 Lia and Aina are the oldest.

Words to Compare Things

Comparatives and superlatives

... (...) more ... (than ...)

The flat is cheaper than the house.

... the most ...

The flat is the cheapest.

... (...) less ... (than ...)

The flat is less cheap than the house.

... the least ...

The flat is the least cheap.

... ... as ... as ...

The flat is as cheap as the house.

The 'el' in ' ' and ' ' has to agree with .

Laura is the shortest.

Jo and Ed are the least tall.

Exceptions

You use ' ' or ' ' with these comparative and superlative forms:

Adjective	Comparative	Superlative
(good)		
(bad)		
(old)		
(young)		

If the noun is or ,
the superlative ' ' changes .
In the , you also need to
to the adjective.

Lia and Aina are the oldest.

Words to Describe Actions

Forming adverbs

There are two ways to form adverbs in Spanish:

1 Add ' .... ' to the end of a .... adjective or an adjective that doesn't end in ' '.

➡️

.... slowly

.... easily

2 Use 'con' and a .... ➡️ con cuidado .... / ....

Adverbs come .... the verb, and they don't need to .... because they're describing an ....

Exceptions

Use ' .... ' to say 'well' and 'mal' to say ' .... '.

.... good ➡️ .... well

malo/a .... ➡️ mal ....

As well as 'rápidamente' and 'lentamente', you can also use ' .... ' and 'despacio' to say 'quickly' and ' .... '.

Adverbs of: **1** time, **2** place and **3** frequency

1

de nuevo	....	de repente	....
....	*already*	....	*now / nowadays*
antes (de)	....	al mismo tiempo	....
después (de)	....	....	*at the moment*
....	*soon*	en seguida	....
....	*still, yet*	mientras tanto	....

2

....	*here*
....	*(just) there*
.... /	*(over) there*
cerca	....
....	*far away*
en / por todas partes	....

3

a diario	....
a menudo	....
....	*sometimes*
siempre	....
de vez en cuando	....
....	*rarely, a few times*

 ☑ ☑ ☑

Topic 11 — Grammar

128

<table>
<tr><td>Second Go:
..... /..... /.....</td><td>**Words to Describe Actions**</td></tr>
</table>

Forming adverbs

There are two ways to form adverbs in Spanish:

1 Add '   ' to the end of a
             or an
        that doesn't end in '   '.   ➡

                                 slowly

                                 easily

2 Use '   ' and a   . ➡   with care / carefully

Adverbs come   the   , and they don't
             because they're describing   .

Exceptions

Use '   ' to say 'well' and '   ' to say 'badly'.

good ➡ well
bad ➡ badly

As well as '   '
and '   ', you
can also use '   '
and '   ' to say
'quickly' and 'slowly'.

Adverbs of: **1** time, **2** place and **3** frequency

1

.... again	.... suddenly
.... already	.... now / nowadays
.... before	.... at the same time
.... after	.... at the moment
.... soon	.... straightaway
.... still, yet	.... meanwhile

2

.... here
.... (just) there
.... / .... (over) there
.... near
.... far away
.... / ....
.... everywhere

3

.... daily
.... often
.... sometimes
.... always
.... from time to time
.... rarely, a few times

Mixed Practice Quizzes

Grammar — everyone's favourite topic. Or is it just mine...? Anyway, it's time to see how well you know p.117-128. Grab a pen and get stuck into these quizzes.

Quiz 1 | Date: ...... / ...... / ......

1) Give the long forms of the possessive adjectives that mean 'my' in Spanish.

2) True or false? You can always tell the gender of nouns ending in '-ista'.

3) How do you say 'four lilac hats' in Spanish?

4) Translate into Spanish: 'Erin is more polite than Eduardo.'

5) 'Hay perros por todas partes.' How would you say this in English?

6) In Spanish, tell your friend that you ate all the grapes.

7) Give the English for: 'No me gustan aquellas faldas.'

8) Translate into English: 'Lo bueno es que puedes visitar a tus abuelos.'

9) Give the plural forms of these Spanish nouns:
   a) la cebolla   b) el papel   c) el pez   d) la nube

10) What does the superlative adjective 'el mayor' mean in English?

Total:

Quiz 2 | Date: ...... / ...... / ......

1) Translate into English: 'Su viejo amigo vive en el centro de Madrid.'

2) Give two words that you can use to say 'quickly' in Spanish.

3) How would you say 'this car' in Spanish?

4) True or false? Indefinite articles are needed after a negative verb.

5) Give the Spanish for: 'There used to be three chairs in the dining room.'

6) What type of adverb are each of these words?
   a) a diario   b) ahí   c) todavía   d) siempre

7) Give the gender of these nouns: 'planeta', 'televisión', 'reportaje', 'igualdad'.

8) 'La próxima vez, no pediremos mariscos.' Say this in English.

9) Say this in Spanish: 'The horse is as friendly as the rabbit.'

10) Give the English for: 'Vuestros abrigos están en el comedor.'

Total:

Mixed Practice Quizzes

Quiz 3   Date: ...... / ...... / ......

1) Turn each of these words into an adverb: 'claro', 'ruidoso', 'curiosidad'.

2) Translate into Spanish: 'The water is very cold today.'

3) Give the English for: 'Creen que la película es peor que el libro.'

4) Give two Spanish nouns that don't follow the usual gender rules.

5) 'I love your (form. sing.) gloves.' How would you say this in Spanish?

6) Which of these sentences is grammatically correct? Explain your answer.
   • Soléis ir al cine los miércoles.   • Odio té, pero bebo café.

7) Explain why adverbs don't need to agree in gender or number.

8) Translate into English: 'Este es el chico cuya casa está al lado de la iglesia.'

9) How would you say you bought a brand-new dishwasher in Spanish?

10) 'Otra mujer dijo que el ladrón era muy alto.' What does this mean?

Total:

Quiz 4   Date: ...... / ...... / ......

1) Write down the plural of these nouns: 'un inglés', 'un joven', 'una canción'.

2) In Spanish, say that Romy is the least talkative.

3) Give the English for: 'Hago las compras cada quince días.'

4) Which of these phrases is grammatically incorrect? Explain your answer.
   • un buen amigo   • la tercera manzana   • alguno día

5) Tell your friend that the roast chicken is the tastiest in Spanish.

6) True or false? Letters of the alphabet are feminine nouns in Spanish.

7) Translate into Spanish: 'These yellow boots are too expensive.'

8) 'El sobrino tuyo es muy sensible.' What does this mean in English?

9) How do you say each of these words and phrases in Spanish?
   a) suddenly   b) far away   c) rarely   d) at the same time

10) How do you make days ending in 's' and surnames plural in Spanish?

Total:

Words to Compare Actions

Comparatives

más ... (que ...)   ... (...)

Eva _____ más alegremente que Inés.
Eva works _____ Inés.

_____ ... (...) less ... (than ...)

Inés _____ alegremente _____ Eva.
Inés works less _____ than Eva.

tan ... como ...   ... _____ ...

Eva _____ tan alegremente como Inés.
Eva _____ Inés.

Superlatives

To say someone does something 'the most / least ...ly', use:

el / la / los / las + _____ + verb + _____ / _____ + adverb

Use either 'el', 'la', 'los' or 'las' to _____ with the _____.

Juan es el _____ trabaja _____ alegremente.
Juan _____ the most _____.

Daniela es la _____ baila _____ energéticamente.
Daniela _____ the least _____.

Irregular forms

Adverb	Comparative	Superlative
bien ( )	(better)	... (the one who ... the best)
mal ( )	(worse)	... (the one who ... the worst)

Cocino _____ mis amigos.   *I _____ better than my friends.*
Ellas son _____ juegan.   *They're the ones who _____ the best.*

Escribes _____ un niño.   *You _____ worse than a _____.*
Él es _____ canta.   *He's the one who _____ the worst.*

Words to Compare Actions

Comparatives

☐ ... (☐ ...) *more ... (than ...)*

Eva works more happily than Inés.

☐ ... (☐ ...) *less ... (than ...)*

Inés works less happily than Eva.

☐ ... ☐ ... *as ... as ...*

Eva works as happily as Inés.

Superlatives

To say someone does something 'the most / least ...ly', use:

☐ / ☐ / ☐ + ☐ + verb + ☐ / ☐ + adverb

Use either ' ☐ ', ' ☐ ', ' ☐ ' or ' ☐ ' to agree with the ☐ .

Juan works the most happily.

Daniela dances the least energetically.

Irregular forms

Adverb	Comparative	Superlative
☐ (well)		
☐ (badly)		

I cook better than my friends.
They're the ones who play the best.

You write worse than a child.
He's the one who sings the worst.

Topic 11 — Grammar

Words to Say How Much

Quantifiers

Use quantifiers before nouns to say [_____] or [_____].
Most change their endings to agree with the noun, but '[_____]' doesn't.

mucho [_____] / [_____]   too much / too many

[_____]   only a little / only a few   [_____]   so much / so many

un poco de [_____]   bastante [_____]

Tenía muchos ....
I had .... lemons.

Hay .... gente.
There are so many ....

Hay .... tarta.
There's a bit of ....

You can also use quantifiers with [_____]. They work like [_____],
so they go after the [_____] and they don't change their [_____].

Hablas ....
You talk too much.

Corre mucho.
She runs ....

[_____]

[_____] strengthen what you're saying. They go [_____] the
word they're modifying, but their [_____] don't [_____] at all.

Simón y Tia están muy felices.
Simón and Tia are ....

Es poco cortés.
He's .... polite.

Habla demasiado tranquilamente.
She ....

Comes bastante bien.
You ....

Making adjectives seem smaller or stronger

You can add '[_____]' to the end of most
adjectives to make something seem smaller or [_____].

El bebé ....
The .... is poorly.

Add '[_____]' to make the
meaning of what you're saying [_____].

La película es ....
The .... is terrible.

Words to Say How Much

Quantifiers

Use quantifiers before _____ to say _____ or how many. Most _____ change their _____ to _____ , but ' _____ ' doesn't.

_____   a lot / lots of   _____   too much / too many

only a little / only a few   _____   so much / so many

_____   a bit of   _____   enough

I had lots of lemons.   There are so many people.   There's a bit of pie.

You can also use quantifiers with _____ . They work like _____ , so they go _____ the _____ and they _____ their _____ .

You talk too much.   She runs a lot.

Intensifiers

Intensifiers _____ what you're saying. They go _____ the _____ word they're _____ , but their endings _____ .

Simón and Tia are very happy.   He's not very polite.

She speaks too quietly.   You eat quite well.

Making adjectives seem smaller or stronger

You can add ' _____ ' to the end of _____ adjectives to make something seem smaller or _____ .   The baby is poorly.

Add ' _____ ' to make the meaning of what you're saying _____ .   The film is terrible.

I, You, We

Subject and object

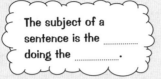
The subject of a sentence is the _____ doing the _____ .

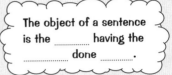
The object of a sentence is the _____ having the _____ done _____ .

' _____ ' is ➡ Pau come la pera. *Pau* _____ *pear.* ⬅ ' _____ '
the subject.   is the object.

I, you, he, she

Pronouns replace _____ . They help to avoid _____ in sentences.

_____ pronouns are words like 'I', 'you', 'he' and 'she'. They're not
normally used in Spanish because _____ show who is doing an action.

I		we	nosotros/as
you (inf. sing.)	tú	you (inf. pl.)	vosotros/as
he / it		they (masc.)	
she / it		they (fem.)	ellas
you (form. sing.)	usted	you (form. pl.)	

⬅ The masculine 'they' form is also used for _____ of masculine and feminine nouns.

Emphasis

Although you don't _____ need subject pronouns in Spanish,
they can help emphasise exactly _____ . They're
used when extra _____ is put on pronouns in English.

¿Qué _____ el fin de semana que viene?
What would you (inf. pl.) like to do _____ ?

Pues, _____ ir de compras, pero él quiere ir al cine.
Well, I want to go _____ *, but* _____ .

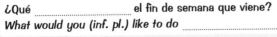

I, You, We

Subject and object

The subject of a sentence is ....

The object of a sentence is ....

'Pau' is the ⟶ [_____] .

Pau eats the pear. ⟵ 'The pear' is the [____] .

I, you, he, she

Pronouns replace [____] . They help to [_____] .

[____] pronouns are words like 'I', 'you', 'he' and 'she'. They're used in Spanish because [_____] show who [_____] .

I		we	
you (inf. sing.)		you (inf. pl.)	
he / it		they (masc.)	
she / it		they (fem.)	
you (form. sing.)		you (form. pl.)	

The masculine 'they' form is also used for .... of masculine and feminine ....

Emphasis

Although you [_____] need [_____] pronouns in Spanish, they can help [_____] .
They're used when [_____] is put on pronouns in English.

What would you (inf. pl.) like to do next weekend?

[_____]

Well, I want to go shopping, but he wants to go to the cinema.

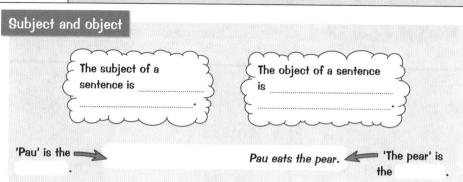

Topic 11 — Grammar

 ☑ ☑ ☑

Me, You, Them

Me, you, him, her

Use direct object pronouns to talk about _____ or _____
an action is _____ . They usually go _____ the verb.

me		us	nos
you (inf. sing.)	te	you (inf. pl.)	
him / it		them (masc.)	
her / it		them (fem.)	
you (form. sing.)	lo/la	you (form. pl.)	los/las

Mika .... el perro.
Mika washes ....

Mika ....
Mika washes it.

To me, to you

Use _____ object pronouns to talk about doing something ' ' or ' '
someone. They're the same pronouns you use with the verb ' _____ '.

to me		to us	nos
to you (inf. sing.)	te	to you (inf. pl.)	
to him / her / it / you (form. sing.)		to them / you (form. pl.)	

El perro da .... a Mika.
The .... gives the brush to Mika.

El perro .... da ....
The .... gives the brush to him.

Order of pronouns

_____ pronouns can go before / after an _____ or a present participle.
You often need to add an _____ to keep the pronunciation the same.

Lo quiero ver. **OR** Quiero verlo.

....

Le estoy hablando. **OR** Estoy hablándole.

....

Pronouns go at the end of ....

Escríbeme. *Write* ....

When two _____ pronouns come together, the _____ one comes first.
The pronouns 'le' or 'les' become ' ' in front of 'lo', 'la', ' ' or ' '.

.... *Give it to him / her / them / you (form.)*

Topic 11 — Grammar

Me, You, Them

Me, you, him, her

Use _____ pronouns to talk about ____ or ____ an action is ____. They usually go ____.

me		us	
you (inf. sing.)		you (inf. pl.)	
him / it		them (masc.)	
her / it		them (fem.)	
you (form. sing.)		you (form. pl.)	

Mika washes the dog.

Mika washes it.

To me, to you

Use _____ pronouns to talk about doing something ' ' or ' ' ____. They're the _____ you use with the verb ' '.

to me		to us	
to you (inf. sing.)		to you (inf. pl.)	
to him / her / it / you (form. sing.)		to them / you (form. pl.)	

The dog gives the brush to Mika. *The dog gives the brush to him.*

Order of pronouns

Object pronouns can go ____ / ____ an ____ or a present ____.
You often need to ____ to keep the ____ the same.

____ / ____
I want to see it.

____ / ____
I'm talking to him.

Pronouns go at the ____ of commands.
Write to me.

When two _____ come together, the indirect one comes ____.
The pronouns ' ' or ' ' become ' ' in front of 'lo', 'la', ' ' or ' '.

Give it to him / her / them / you (form.)

  ☑ ☑ 😊 ☑

More Pronouns

Que

'Que' can mean '_____', 'which' or 'who' — it's a _____ pronoun. Use it to start a _____ clause, which is a way of adding _____ to a sentence.

¿Dónde está _____ que _____? *Where is the bread _____ you bought?*

To talk about an _____ instead of an object, you need '_____ que'.

Van a venir, _____ que es genial. _____, *which is great.*

After _____, like 'con', 'a' and '_____', use 'quien(es)' for _____ (who) and 'el / la / los / las que' or 'el / la / los / las cual(es)' for _____ (that / which).

_____ con quien estoy hablando
the man with _____

el mercado del cual _____
the market _____ I buy flowers

(With) me and (with) you

After _____ like 'a', '_____', 'sobre' and '_____', the words for 'me' and 'you (inf. sing.)' become '_____' and '_____'. '_____' needs an accent.

Es para ti. *It's _____.*

'_____' becomes 'conmigo' and
'_____' becomes 'contigo'.

Está conmigo. *He's _____.*

Indefinite pronouns

'Algo' (_____) and 'alguien' (_____) are indefinite pronouns.

¿Quieren algo?
Do they _____?

Vi a alguien. _____.

You need the personal 'a' when you _____ in Spanish.

Interrogative pronouns

Use '_____' (what) to ask about a specific thing or idea. Use '_____' or '_____' (which) to distinguish between two or more things.

¿_____ haces? *What are _____?*   ¿_____ es? *Which (one) _____?*

'_____' means 'Who...' and is often used with _____.

¿Con _____? *With whom?*

More Pronouns

Que

'Que' can mean '   ', '   ' or '   ' — it's a   .
Use it to start a   clause, which is a way of   a sentence.

Where is the bread that you bought?

To talk about an   instead of an   , you need '   '.

They're going to come, which is great.

After   , like 'con', 'a' and 'de', use
'   ' for   (who) and 'el / la / los / las que' or
'el / la / los / las   ' for   (that / which).

the man with whom I'm talking

the market from which I buy flowers

(With) me and (with) you

After   like 'a', '   ',
'   ' and 'de', the words for
'me' and 'you (inf. sing.)' become
'   ' and '   '. '   ' needs an   .

It's for you.

'With me' becomes '   ' and
'with you' becomes '   '.

He's with me.

pronouns

'   ' (something) and '   '
(someone) are   pronouns.

Do they want something?

I saw someone.

You need the ....
when you 'see someone' in Spanish.

Interrogative pronouns

Use '   ' (what) to ask about a   or idea. Use '   '
or '   ' (which) to   two or more things.

What are you doing?

Which (one) is it?

'   ' means 'Who...' and
is often used with   .

With whom?

More Pronouns

_____ pronouns

Use _____ pronouns to say who something _____ to.
They agree in _____ and number with the _____ they're replacing.

	Masc. sing.	Fem. sing.	Masc. pl.	Fem. pl.
mine			los míos	las mías
yours (inf. sing.)		la tuya		las tuyas
his / hers / its / yours (form. sing.)	el suyo			
ours		la nuestra	los nuestros	
yours (inf. pl.)	el vuestro			las vuestras
theirs / yours (form. pl.)			los suyos	

¿Es tu casa? No, _____ es más alta. Is it _____? No, mine _____.

¿Es su hotel? No, _____ está allí. Is it _____? No, ours _____.

_____ pronouns

_____ pronouns look the same as demonstrative adjectives.
Their _____ change to agree with the _____ they refer back to.

	Masc. sing.	Fem. sing.	Masc. pl.	Fem. pl.
this / these one(s)			estos	
that / those one(s)	ese			
that / those one(s) over there				aquellas

Me gustaría _____.
I _____ this one.

Prefiere _____.
She _____ those.

Compré _____.
I _____ those over there.

Use the neuter forms 'esto', '_____' and '_____'
if you don't know the _____ of the noun.

¿Qué es _____? What's that?

142

More Pronouns

Possessive pronouns

Use possessive pronouns to say _____ .
They agree in _____ and _____ with the _____ .

Possessive	Masc. sing.	Fem. sing.	Masc. pl.	Fem. pl.
mine				
yours (inf. sing.)				
his / hers / its / yours (form. sing.)				
ours				
yours (inf. pl.)				
theirs / yours (form. pl.)				

Is it your house? No, mine is taller.

Is it your hotel? No, ours is there.

Demonstrative pronouns

Demonstrative pronouns look the same as _____ .
Their _____ change to _____ they _____ .

Demonstrative	Masc. sing.	Fem. sing.	Masc. pl.	Fem. pl.
this / these one(s)				
that / those one(s)				
that / those one(s) over there				

I would like this one.   *She prefers those.*   *I bought those over there.*

Use the neuter forms ' ____ ', ' ____ ' and ' _____ '
if you don't know _____ .

What's that?

Mixed Practice Quizzes

After those pages, I'm sure you're raring to go with some more quizzes. See what you can remember from p.131-142 with these ones, and jot down your scores.

Quiz 1 Date: ...... / ...... / ......

1) True or false? Quantifiers have to agree when they're used with verbs.
2) In Spanish, which subject pronoun refers to a group of men and women?
3) Translate into Spanish: 'She is the one who plays the piano the best.'
4) Give the English for: 'No entiendo lo que dijiste.'
5) How do you say 'with you' in Spanish?
6) 'Hay tantas flores en el jardín.' Say this in English.
7) What are pronouns used for?
8) True or false? After 'sobre', the word for 'me' becomes 'mí'.
9) Give the English for: 'Os mando un mensaje sobre la fiesta.'
10) Replace each noun below with the correct possessive pronoun for 'hers'.
   a) la manzana   b) los barcos   c) el perro   d) las canciones

Total:

Quiz 2 Date: ...... / ...... / ......

1) 'Iria añade la nata.' What is the object in this sentence?
2) True or false? 'Poco' can be used as a quantifier and an intensifier.
3) Translate into Spanish: 'Jimena cocina la comida italiana mejor que Ian.'
4) What are the four subject pronouns for 'you' in Spanish?
5) Give the English for: 'Quiero un nuevo abrigo. Me gusta este.'
6) Change this sentence so that it means 'We bought it for our friend.':
   'Compramos la bolsa para nuestro amigo.'
7) True or false? Object pronouns can only go before an infinitive.
8) Give the English for: 'Conduce tan lentamente como Benat.'
9) 'Is it her car? No, hers is blue.' Say this in Spanish.
10) What type of pronoun is 'que'?

Total:

Mixed Practice Quizzes

Date: ...... / ...... / ......

1) Give the English for: 'Juegas al fútbol peor que yo.'
2) Why are subject pronouns used in this sentence?
   'A ellos les gusta el brócoli, pero yo pienso que es horrible.'
3) Give the English for: 'Estos libros son los vuestros.'
4) Which interrogative pronoun would you use to ask about a specific thing?
5) True or false? Adding 'ísimo' to an adjective makes the meaning stronger.
6) Translate into English: 'Esos son los más caros.'
7) 'We speak the most calmly.' Say this in Spanish.
8) Which of the following would be used to say 'from which' after 'la tienda'?
   • del cual   • de que   • de la cual   • de quien
9) In Spanish, which indirect object pronoun would you use to say 'to them'?
10) How do you say 'Yanfei come demasiado rápidamente' in English?

Total:

Date: ...... / ...... / ......

1) What type of words are 'algo' and 'alguien'?
2) Give the English for: 'Mi sobrina es bajita y graciosa.'
3) Translate into Spanish: 'I eat too much chocolate.'
4) Where do pronouns go in a command?
5) Translate into English: '¿Con quién te vas de vacaciones?'
6) True or false? Subject pronouns aren't used much in Spanish.
7) Say these sentences in Spanish, using feminine demonstrative pronouns.
   a) I want those.   b) We prefer these.   c) She sees those over there.
8) Which of these sentences uses pronouns in the correct order?
   • La me vendieron.   • Me la vendieron.   • Me vendieron la.
9) Give the English for: 'Cantan menos dulcemente que tú.'
10) Translate into Spanish: 'I need a laptop. I will buy that one over there.'

Total:

Prepositions

Common prepositions

	between
bajo / debajo de	
	above / on top of
	against
al fondo de	
	towards
sin	
según	

▬▬ , ▬▬

For 'on top of', use '_____' or '_____'.

Está _____ la mesa.
It's on the table.

For 'on' but not 'on top of', use '_____'.

Lo vi _____ la tele. *I saw it on TV.*

You don't need '_____' _____...
for days of the week. *On Monday...*

De

Use 'de' to mean '_____' or to say what something is made of.

Es de oro. *It's _____ gold.*

You can't say 'de el' (or 'a el'):

	el	la
de		de la
a		a la

En, a

You normally use 'en' to say '_____', but sometimes you need 'a'.

Está en el cañón.
She's _____.

a las seis _____

al final de _____

En, dentro de

Use 'en' to say '_____' and 'dentro de' to say '_____'. The verb '_____' is normally followed by 'en'.

En Leeds...
_____ Leeds...

dentro de la caja
_____ the box

_____ en la tienda. *I enter the shop.*

A, hasta

Use '_____' to say 'to'. When 'to' means 'as far as', use '_____'.

Va _____ Liverpool.
She is going to Liverpool.

Solo va _____ Manchester.
He is only going to Manchester.

De, desde, a partir de

'From' is usually '_____'. Use '_____' with a start and end point and '_____' for dates.

Es _____ Kent.
He's from Kent.

_____ Fife hasta Ayr   from Fife _____ Ayr

_____ Julio   *from* _____

 ☑ ☑ ☑

Topic 11 — Grammar

Prepositions

Common prepositions

between

below / under

above / on top of

against

at the back of

towards

without

according to

Sobre, en

For ' _____ ', use 'sobre' or 'en'.

It's on the table.

For ' _____ ' but not ' _____ ', use 'en'.

I saw it on TV.

You don't need ' _____ ' for

_____ . On Monday...

Use ' _____ ' to mean 'of' or to say

_____ .

It's made of gold.

You can't say
' _____ '

(or ' _____ '):

	el	la
de		
a		

You normally use ' _____ ' to say 'at',
but sometimes you need ' _____ '.

She's at the canyon.

at six o'clock

at the end of

Use ' _____ ' to say 'in' and ' _____ '
to say 'inside'. The verb 'entrar'
is normally followed by ' _____ '.

In Leeds...   inside the box

I enter the shop.

A, _____

Use 'a' to say ' _____ '. When ' _____ '
means 'as far as', use ' _____ '.

She is going to Liverpool.

He is only going to Manchester.

De, desde, a partir de

' _____ ' is usually 'de'. Use 'desde' with a
and 'a partir de' for _____ .

He's from Kent.   from Fife to Ayr   from July

'Por', 'Para' and the Personal 'a'

First Go:
..... / ..... / .....

Use 'por' to...

1 ...talk about [   ] duration.   Vivió allí por un año.

2 ...talk about parts of the [   ].   por la mañana

3 ...say '[   ]'.   Entré por la puerta.

4 ...say '[   ]' or '[   ]' in number phrases.   una vez por día

5 ...talk about [   ].   Pagué por el té.

6 ...say 'on [   ] of'.   Lo hice por ti.

7 ...say '[   ]'.   Gracias por el boli.

Use 'para' to...

1 ...say _____ something is for.   Este bote es para ti.

2 ...talk about _____.   el tren para Bilbao

3 ...say '_____' or '_____'.   Corro para descansar.

4 ...say '_____' in time phrases.   para mañana

5 ...talk about _____ duration.   Lo quiero para un día.

6 ...give an _____.   Para mí, es bonito.

7 ...say '_____'.   Está para llover.

The personal 'a'

You need an extra 'a' before the word for any
[   ] or [   ] after almost every verb.

You don't usually use the personal 'a' after '_____' or '_____'.

Estoy buscando _____.   **BUT**   Estoy buscando _____.
I'm looking for Rhea.   *I'm looking for a taxi.*

 ☑   ☑   ☑

Topic 11 — Grammar

'Por', 'Para' and the Personal 'a'

Use '_____' to...

1 ...talk about _____ . *He lived there for a year.*

2 ...talk about _____ . *in the morning*

3 ...say '_____'. *I came through the door.*

4 ...say '____' or 'a' in number phrases. *once a day*

5 ...talk about _____ . *I paid for the tea.*

6 ...say _____ . *I did it for you.*

7 ...say _____ . *Thanks for the pen.*

Use '_____' to...

1 ...say _____ . *This jar is for you.*

2 ...talk about _____ . *the train for Bilbao*

3 ...say '_____' or '_____'. *I run to relax.*

4 ...say '_____' in _____ phrases. *by tomorrow*

5 ...talk about _____ . *I want it for one day.*

6 ...give an _____ . *For me, it's pretty.*

7 ...say '_____'. *It's about to rain.*

The personal '⬤'

You need an extra '____' before the word for any _____ or pet after almost every _____ .

You _____ use the personal 'a' after _____ or _____ .

I'm looking for Rhea. **BUT** *I'm looking for a taxi.*

Conjunctions

Y

'Y' means ' '.

Juego al fútbol y al rugby.
....

'Y' changes to ' ' before a word starting with ' ' or ' '.

Hablo español ...... inglés.
....

O

'O' means ' '.

.... fútbol o al rugby los sábados.
I play football ...... rugby ....

'O' changes to ' ' before a word starting with ' ' or ' '.

Cuesta siete ...... ocho euros.
....

Pero

'Pero' means ' '.

Me gusta el fútbol, pero no me gusta el rugby.
....

Use 'sino' when you want to say ' '.

No es español, sino francés.
....

Porque

'Porque' helps you give .

Me gusta porque es sabroso.
....

Other common conjunctions

sin embargo

so, therefore

de manera que

mientras

as, since

pues

entonces

cuando

as, because

if

Conjunctions

' ⬜ ' means 'and'.

> *I play football and rugby.*

' ⬜ ' changes to 'e' before a word starting with ' ⬜ ' or ' ⬜ '.

> *I speak Spanish and English.*

' ⬜ ' means 'or'.

> *I play football or rugby on Saturdays.*

' ⬜ ' changes to 'u' before a word starting with ' ⬜ ' or ' ⬜ '.

> *It costs seven or eight euros.*

' ⬜ ' means 'but'.

> *I like football, but I don't like rugby.*

Use ' ⬜ ' when you want to say 'but rather'.

> *He isn't Spanish, but (rather) French.*

Porque

'Porque' helps you ⬜ .

> *I like it because it's tasty.*

Other common conjunctions

⬜	however	⬜	as, because
⬜	so, therefore	⬜	well, then
⬜	such that	⬜	then
⬜	while	⬜	if
	as, since	⬜	when

Verbs in the Present Tense

Forming the present tense

Most regular verbs in Spanish end in '-____', '-er' or '-____'.
To form the present tense, you need to find the stem.
To do this, remove the last [____] letters from the infinitive.   hablar ➡

Then add the endings below to the stem:

-ar verbs, e.g. '[____]'	
	hablamos
hablas	
habla	

Cantan bien.
.... *well.*

Echo la pelota.
.... *the ball.*

-er verbs, e.g. '[____]'	
como	
	coméis
come	

Bebes té.
.... *tea.*

Vendemos uvas.
.... *grapes.*

-ir verbs, e.g. '[____]'	
vivo	
vives	
	viven

Interrumpís.
....

Linh escribe una carta.
.... *a letter.*

Use the present tense...

1 ...for actions taking place [____].   Estudio español.   .... *Spanish.*

2 ...for things that take place [____].   .... cada día.   *I cook every day.*

3 ...with [____] to say how long you've been doing something.

Toco el violín .... un año.   .... *the violin for one year.*

4 ...for things that are [____] to happen.   Mañana vamos ....
Tomorrow .... *to the beach.*

 ✓   ✓   ✓

Topic 11 — Grammar

Verbs in the Present Tense

Forming the present tense

Most regular verbs in Spanish end in '-   ', '-   ' or '-   '.
To form the present tense, you need to find the   .
To do this, remove   from the   .

Then add the endings below to the   :

hablar ➡

-ar verbs, e.g. 'hablar'	

They sing well.

I throw the ball.

-er verbs, e.g. 'comer'	

You drink tea.

We sell grapes.

-ir verbs, e.g. 'vivir'	

You interrupt.

Linh writes a letter.

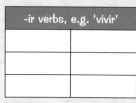

Use the present tense...

1 ...for   taking place   .

I study Spanish.

2 ...for things that take place   .

I cook every day.

3 ...with '   ' to say   you've been doing something.

I've been playing the violin for one year.

4 ...for things that are
                              .

Tomorrow we are going to the beach.

Irregular Verbs in the Present Tense

Radical-changing verbs

These verbs use _____ verb endings but change their spelling in the present tense in every form apart from the '_____' and '_____' forms.

The 'e' to 'i' change only happens in '_____' verbs.

'e' to 'ie', e.g. querer	
	queremos
quiere	quieren

'o/u' to 'ue', e.g. poder	
puedo	
puedes	podéis

'e' to 'i', e.g. pedir	
	pedimos
pides	
pide	

Other 'e' to 'ie' verbs:

....	to close
comenzar	....
....	to begin
....	to think
....	to prefer
sentir(se)	....
tener	....
venir	....

Other 'o/u' to 'ue' verbs:

costar	....
....	to hurt
dormir	....
encontrar	....
....	to play
....	to rain
morir	....
....	to return

Other 'e' to 'i' verbs:

conseguir	....
....	to correct
elegir	....
....	to measure
....	to repeat
seguir	....
....	to serve
sonreírse	....

The _____ forms of 'tener' and 'venir' are _____ .

Common irregular verbs

Irregular forms:

'Ir' (_____): completely irregular.

vas	vais
va	

'Dar' (_____): the '_____' form ('doy') and the '_____' form ('dais').

Te doy el libro. .... the book.

'Hacer' (_____): the '_____' form ('hago').

Hago la cama. .... the bed.

'Saber' (_____): the '_____' form ('sé').

Sé su edad. .... her age.

'Conocer' (_____): the '_____' form ('conozco').

Conozco a Abir. .... Abir.

Irregular Verbs in the Present Tense

Radical-changing verbs

These verbs use [_____] verb endings but change their [_____] in the present tense in every form apart from the '[_____]' and '[_____]' forms.

The .... change only happens in '............' verbs.

'e' to '⬤', e.g. querer		'o/u' to '⬤', e.g. poder		'e' to '⬤', e.g. pedir	

Other 'e' to '__' verbs:

to close
to begin
to begin
to think
to prefer
to feel
to have
to come

Other 'o/u' to '__' verbs:

to cost
to hurt
to sleep
to find
to play
to rain
to die
to return

Other 'e' to '__' verbs:

to achieve
to correct
to choose
to measure
to repeat
to follow
to serve
to smile

The first person singular forms of '[_____]' and '[_____]' are irregular.

Common irregular verbs

Irregular forms:

'[_____]' (to go): [_____] irregular.

'[_____]' (to do / make): the 'I' form ('[_____]').

I make the bed.

'[_____]' (to know, e.g. [_____]): the 'I' form ('[____]').

I know her age.

'[_____]' (to give): the 'I' form ('[____]') and the 'you (inf. pl.)' form ('[_____]').

I give you the book.

'[_____]' (to know, e.g. [_____]): the 'I' form ('[_____]').

I know Abir.

'Ser' and 'Estar' in the Present Tense

'Ser' means ' [____] '

'Ser' is for [_____] things.
It's a completely irregular verb.

ser ([____])	
	somos
es	son

Use it to...

1 ...talk about [_____].

Somos galeses. .... Welsh.

2 ...say someone's [_____]
or who they are.

Nerea .... mi prima.   *Nerea is my cousin.*

3 ...talk about someone's [____].

Mi tío es profesor.   *My uncle .... teacher.*

4 ...describe [_____] characteristics.

.... altos.   *You (inf. pl.) are tall.*

5 ...describe someone's [_____].

.... alegres.   *They are cheerful.*

'Estar' means ' [____] '

'Estar' is for [_____]
things and locations. It's a
completely irregular verb.

estar ([____])	
estoy	
estás	
está	

Use it to...

1 ...talk about things that [_____] in the future.

Estoy .... enfermo.
.... *quite ill.*

Estás muy triste.   .... *very sad.*

2 ...talk about [_____] someone or something is.

Madrid .... en España.
Madrid is in Spain.

.... en casa.   *We are ....*

'Ser' and 'Estar' in the Present Tense

'Ser' means 'to be'

'Ser' is for [_____] things.
It's a [_____] verb.

ser (to be)	

Use it to...

1 ...talk about [_____].   *We are Welsh.*

2 ...say someone's [_____]
or [_____].   *Nerea is my cousin.*

3 ...talk about someone's [____].   *My uncle is a teacher.*

4 ...describe [_____] characteristics.   *You (inf. pl.) are tall.*

5 ...describe someone's [_____].   *They are cheerful.*

'Estar' means 'to be'

'Estar' is for [_____]
things and [_____]. It's
a [_____] verb.

estar (to be)	

Use it to...

1 ...talk about things that might [_____] in the [_____].

I'm quite ill.   *You are very sad.*

2 ...talk about [_____].

Madrid is in Spain.   *We are at home.*

Mixed Practice Quizzes

I don't know about you, but I fancy a quiz break. These questions will test you on p.145-156. Have a go at each quiz, then check to see how well you did.

Quiz 1 Date: ...... / ...... / ......

1) Explain how you find the stem of a Spanish verb.
2) How would you translate the underlined words into Spanish?
   a) The book is <u>on</u> the chair.   b) The jacket is <u>made of</u> leather.
3) 'Trabajé en la tienda por tres meses.' Why is 'por' used in this sentence?
4) True or false? 'Ser' and 'estar' are both completely irregular verbs.
5) Give the Spanish for: 'We swim in the river every day.'
6) How does the stem of the verb 'corregir' change in the present tense?
7) 'He saves money in order to go on holiday.' Say this in Spanish.
8) Translate into English: 'Según ella, el problema es muy grave.'
9) Say this in Spanish: 'I have been to Scotland and Ireland.'
10) How would you say 'from September' in Spanish?

Total:

Quiz 2 Date: ...... / ...... / ......

1) Translate into Spanish: 'You (inf. sing.) are at the bus station.'
2) Say this in English: 'Preparo la cena mientras los niños ven la televisión.'
3) 'Caminan hasta el bosque antes de volver a casa.' Say this in English.
4) Tell your friend that you know Sergio because he's your uncle in Spanish.
5) Translate into English: 'Creo que está para nevar.'
6) Give the Spanish for: 'Her stepmother is a postwoman.'
7) 'Vivís allí desde hace cinco años.' What does this mean in English?
8) True or false? You should use 'estar' to describe someone's personality.
9) Translate into Spanish: 'The cat sleeps on the armchair.'
10) '¿La bufanda es azul claro u oscuro?' Say this in English.

Total:

Mixed Practice Quizzes

Quiz 3 Date: ...... / ...... / ......

1) Give the irregular present tense forms of the verb 'dar'.

2) Translate into English: '¿Cómo accedes las redes sociales?'

3) Explain why there is a preposition after the verb in this sentence: 'La semana pasada, vió a Angela en los grandes almacenes.'

4) Conjugate the verb 'leer' in the present tense.

5) Give the English for: 'Había cien euros dentro de mi bolso.'

6) 'Abdel and Iñigo are my best friends.' How would you say this in Spanish?

7) 'Sin embargo, usted no está de acuerdo con la decisión.' How would you say this in English?

8) Translate into English: 'Vi un pájaro enorme encima de los árboles.'

9) Give the English for: 'Vendo periódicos los fines de semana.'

10) 'My father isn't a builder, but rather a baker.' Say this in Spanish.

Total:

Quiz 4 Date: ...... / ...... / ......

1) Translate into English: 'Como no sabía la respuesta, no le respondí.'

2) How does the stem of the verb 'encontrar' change in the present tense?

3) Give the Spanish for: 'I lost my suitcase at the airport.'

4) 'Thank you for helping us with the homework.' Say this in Spanish.

5) Conjugate the verbs 'ser' and 'estar' in the present tense.

6) Translate into Spanish: 'This afternoon I am buying a new watch.'

7) Which sentence below is grammatically correct? Explain your answer.
   - Buscan a Rover, su perro blanco.
   - Miran a las fotos del bebé.

8) Correct the errors in this sentence: 'Abriré la puerta a el final de el pasillo.'

9) Give the infinitive of these conjugated radical-changing verbs:
   a) consiguen   b) cierras   c) duele   d) comienza

10) 'It is quite hot in the kitchen.' How would you say this in Spanish?

Total:

Talking About the Past

The preterite tense

To form the preterite tense of .... verbs,
find the .... and then add these endings:

-ar verbs	
-é	
	-asteis
-ó	

-er and -ir verbs	
	-imos
-iste	
	-ieron

.... el arroz.
They cooked the ....

.... la ventana.
I opened ....

Irregular verbs

' .... ',' .... ',' .... ' and 'hacer' are the four most important irregular verbs
in the preterite tense. ' .... ' and ' .... ' are the same in the preterite tense.

⬤(to be), ⬤(to go)	
fui	
	fueron

⬤(to be)	
estuviste	estuvisteis

hacer (to ⬤/⬤)	
	hicimos
hizo	

Verbs ending in '-car' change their 'c' to ' .... ' in the ' ' form.   tocar ➡ ....

Verbs ending in '-zar' change their 'z' to ' .... ' in the ' ' form.   cruzar ➡ ....

Some verbs change their .... in the preterite tense, and they also
lose the .... on their ' .... ' and 'he/she/it/you (form. sing.)' forms.

dar (to give)	
.... (to say)	dij-
.... (to be able to)	pud-
poner (to put)	

querer (.........)	
tener (.........)	
.... (to bring)	traj-
venir (to come)	

Lo .... en la mesa.
We put it ....

.... a la fiesta.
You came to ....

Mia me .... un gato.
Mia gave me ....

 ☑ ☑ ☑

Talking About the Past

The preterite tense

To form the preterite tense of .... verbs,
find the .... and then .... :

-ar verbs	

-er and -ir verbs	

They cooked the rice.

I opened the window.

Irregular verbs

' ..... ', ' ..... ', ' .... ' and ' .... ' are the four most important irregular verbs
in the preterite tense. ' ..... ' and ' ..... ' are the same in the preterite tense.

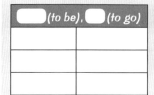

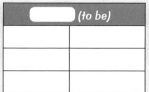

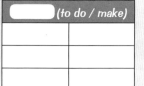

Verbs ending in ' ..... ' change their 'c' to ' ..... ' in the ' ..... ' form.   tocar ➡

Verbs ending in ' ..... ' change their 'z' to ' ..... ' in the ' ..... ' form.   cruzar ➡

Some verbs change .... in the preterite tense, and they also
.... on their ' ..... ' and 'he/she/it/you (form. sing.)' forms.

(to give)	
(to say)	
(to be able to)	
(to put)	

(to want)	
(to have)	
(to bring)	
(to come)	

We put it on the table.

You came to the party.

Mia gave me a cat.

     ✓   ✓   ✓

Talking About the Past

The imperfect tense

To form the imperfect tense, find the [____] and then add [_____] :

-ar verbs	
	-abais
-aba	

-er and -ir verbs	
-ía	
	-ían

The '____' form and the 'he/she/it/you (form. sing.)' form look the same.

_____ Iratxe.
I was talking to Iratxe.

_____ en el cine.
You were _____ .

Iris _____ hambre.
Iris was _____ .

_____ allí.
We used to live _____ .

[_____] verbs

'Ser' and 'ir' are completely [_____] . '[____]' uses the regular [_____] tense endings but has an irregular [____], 've-'.

ser ([____])	
era	
era	

ir ([____])	
ibas	ibais

ver ([____])	
	veíamos
	veían

_____ era pintor.
My dad _____ .

_____ al concierto.
We went _____ .

_____ la tele.
I used to watch TV.

Había

'Había' is the imperfect form of '[____]'.
It means '[_____]' or '[_____]'.

'_____' and 'había' come from the verb '_____'

It stays the same regardless of whether the noun is [_____] or [_____] .

Había _____ en el árbol.
_____ a monkey in _____ .

Siempre había _____ .
_____ always lots of children there.

Talking About the Past

The imperfect tense

To form the imperfect tense, [ ] and then [ ] :

-ar verbs	

-er and -ir verbs	

The ' ...... ' form and the
'he/she/it/you (form. sing.)'
form ....

I was talking to Iratxe.

Iris was hungry.

You were at the cinema.

We used to live there.

[ ] verbs

' [ ] ' and ' [ ] ' are completely [ ] . 'Ver' uses the regular
[ ] but has an irregular [ ] , ' [ ] '.

[ ] (to be)	

[ ] (to go)	

[ ] (to see)	

My dad was a painter.

We went to the concert.

I used to watch TV.

[ ]

' [ ] ' is the imperfect form of 'hay'.
It means ' [ ] ' or ' [ ] '.

It stays [ ] regardless of whether [ ] is [ ] or [ ] .

'Hay' and ' .... ' come
from the verb ' .... '.

There was a monkey in the tree.

There were always lots of children there.

Talking About the Past

Use the preterite tense to...

1 ...talk about a single .... in the past.

Fui a la playa ....
I .... on Thursday.

2 ...talk about events that happened during a .... of time.

Ayer hizo calor.
Yesterday ....

3 ...interrupt a description of .... taking place in the .... tense.

.... del gimnasio cuando ..... a Delaram.
I was coming back .... when I saw Delaram.

Use the imperfect tense to...

1 ...talk about what you .... do .... in the past.

Iba a .... cada día.
I .... go to the beach ....

You can also use 'solía' (the .... tense of '............')
and an .... to say what you used to do.

Solía ..... a .... cada día. I .... go to the beach ....

2 ....,
like the weather, in the past.

............................, pero estaba nublado.
It was hot, but ....

3 ...say where you .... going when .... happened.

.... del gimnasio cuando ..... a Delaram.
I was coming back .... when I saw Delaram.

4 ...say .... something had been happening for with 'desde hacía' (the imperfect form of '............').

Leía desde hacía una hora cuando me llamó.
I .... for an hour when he ....

Topic 11 — Grammar

Talking About the Past

Use the preterite tense to...

1 ...talk about a single _____ .

> I went to the beach on Thursday.

2 ...talk about events that _____ during _____ .

> Yesterday it was hot.

3 ... _____ a description of _____ taking place in the _____ tense.

> I was coming back from the gym when I saw Delaram.

Use the imperfect tense to...

1 ...talk about what you _____ .

> I used to go to the beach every day.

You can also use ' _____ ' (the imperfect tense of 'soler')
and _____ to say _____ .

> I used to go to the beach every day.

2 ...describe something, like _____ , in the _____ . It was hot, but it was cloudy.

3 ...say where you _____ when _____ .

> I was coming back from the gym when I saw Delaram.

4 ...say _____ something had _____ with 'desde hacía' (the imperfect form of ' _____ ').

> Leía desde hacía una hora cuando me llamó.

Talking About the Past

Past participles

In the sentence 'I have done', 'done' is a past participle.
Past participles _____ have to agree when used as part of a _____.
To form a past participle, find the _____, then add these endings:

-ar verbs		-er verbs		-ir verbs	

hablar ....   beber ....   elegir ....

There are some _____ participles that you also need to learn:

abrir _____ *(opened)*   leído (_____)

cubrir _____ (_____)   poner _____ *(put)*

_____ dicho *(said)*   roto (_____)

_____ escrito (_____)   ver _____ (_____)

hacer _____ *(done / made)*   volver _____ *(returned)*

The perfect tense

Use the perfect tense to talk about what you '_____'.
You need the present tense of the verb '_____' and a _____ participle.

_____ — present tense	
has	
	han

Han ....   *They have played tennis.*

¡Ojas .... la llave!   *Ojas has broken .... !*

The pluperfect tense

Use the pluperfect tense to talk about what you '_____'.
You need the imperfect tense of the verb '_____' and a _____ participle.

_____ — imperfect tense	
	habíamos
	habían

.... un gato.   *She had bought a cat.*

Habían .... el coche.   *They had seen ....*

Talking About the Past

Past participles

In the sentence 'I have done', '⬚' is a past participle.
Past participles don't ⬚ when used as ⬚.
To form a past participle, ⬚, then ⬚:

| -ar verbs | ⬚ | -er verbs | ⬚ | -ir verbs | ⬚ |

| hablar | beber | elegir |

There are some ⬚ that you also need to learn:

⬚	⬚	*(opened)*	⬚	*(read)*
		(covered)	⬚	*(put)*
decir	⬚	*(said)*		*(broken)*
		(written)		*(seen)*
		(done / made)		*(returned)*

The perfect tense

Use the perfect tense to talk about ⬚.
You need the present tense of the verb '⬚' and ⬚.

⬚ — present tense	

They have played tennis.

Ojas has broken the key!

The pluperfect tense

Use the pluperfect tense to talk about ⬚.
You need the imperfect tense of the verb '⬚' and ⬚.

⬚ — imperfect tense	

She had bought a cat.

They had seen the car.

Mixed Practice Quizzes

Unfortunately you can't put past tenses behind you just yet — you need to make sure they won't fade from your memory. Try these quizzes about p.159-166.

Quiz 1 | Date: ...... / ...... / ......

1) Give two uses of the preterite tense.

2) Translate into English: 'Hemos visto todas sus películas y nos encantan.'

3) Give the Spanish for: 'You (inf. pl.) were driving to the town centre.'

4) True or false? '-ar' and '-er' verbs use the same preterite tense endings.

5) Give two uses of the imperfect tense.

6) Give the English for: 'Íbamos al zoo cuando el tigre se escapó.'

7) 'Veíamos un partido de rugby en el estadio.' Say this in English.

8) Explain how verbs ending in '-car' and '-zar' change in the 'I' form of the preterite tense.

9) Give the Spanish for: 'There was a cake on the table.'

10) How do you say 'They had cooked dinner together' in Spanish?

Total:

Quiz 2 | Date: ...... / ...... / ......

1) Translate into English: '¿Habéis leído el libro? Trata de una periodista.'

2) Give the stem of each of these verbs in the preterite tense.
   a) tener   b) quedar   c) querer   d) vivir   e) poner

3) Give the Spanish for: 'You (inf. sing.) wrote the letter to your cousin.'

4) What is the past participle of 'cubrir'?

5) Give two ways you could say 'I used to sing' in Spanish.

6) Translate into English: 'Había dos pájaros en la tienda.'

7) Conjugate the verb 'beber' in the imperfect tense.

8) Explain how you form a regular past participle in Spanish.

9) True or false? 'Ser' and 'ir' are the same in the preterite tense.

10) Translate into Spanish: 'I was walking home when I received your message.'

Total:

Mixed Practice Quizzes

Quiz 3   Date: ...... / ...... / ......

1) Give the Spanish for: 'You (form. sing.) have put the pen in your rucksack.'

2) 'I looked for a cardigan because I was cold.' Say this in Spanish.

3) Should this sentence use the preterite or the imperfect tense in Spanish?
   'It was stormy last weekend.'

4) Which of the following translates as 'They were running'?
   • Corrimos   • Corrábamos   • Corríamos   • Corramos

5) Translate into English: 'Habíamos hecho las compras.'

6) Conjugate the verb 'estar' in the preterite tense.

7) What are the past participles of these verbs?
   a) tocar   b) abrir   c) beber   d) volver

8) True or false? 'Hacer' is irregular in the imperfect tense.

9) Put this sentence in the preterite tense: 'Hago deportes acuáticos.'

10) Give the Spanish for: 'They went to the park to play football.'

Total:

Quiz 4   Date: ...... / ...... / ......

1) Translate into English: 'Nos trajeron algunos regalos.'

2) 'Solía escuchar música pop.' Say this in English.

3) What does 'Mi abuela era jugadora de tenis' mean in English?

4) True or false? The perfect tense uses the imperfect tense of 'haber'.

5) Translate into Spanish: 'I organised the event with the youth club.'

6) Which of these sentences is in the preterite tense?
   • Pagabas la cuenta.   • Te gustó el libro.   • Me habías ayudado.

7) Give the Spanish for: 'Álvaro travelled to Spain to visit his friend.'

8) What is the past participle of the verb 'romper'?

9) How do you say 'We used to dance every Friday' in Spanish?

10) 'Aprendías español desde hacía cuatro años.' Say this in English.

Total:

Talking About the Future

The immediate future tense

Use the immediate future tense to talk about _____ as well as something further in the future.

| present tense of ' ( ) ' | + | a | + | ( ) |

Me voy a comer la pera.
_____ the pear.

Susana _____ una revista.
Susana is going to read a magazine.

Add time phrases to say _____ something.

_____, vamos a ir a Francia.
On Monday, _____ to France.

Mañana _____ .
_____ I'm going to swim.

The proper future tense

Use the proper future tense to say _____ .

 ( ) + future tense endings

-ar, -er and -ir verbs	
	-emos
-ás	

Jugaré al tenis. _____ tennis.

_____ el autobús. *He will take the bus.*

Venderán el perro. _____ the dog.

Some verbs have a special future _____ :

(to say)	dir-	querer (to want)		
haber (to have...)		( )	sabr-
hacer (to do / make)		(to come)	
(to have)	tendr-	salir ( )	
poner ( )		(to be able to)	podr-

Lo _____ mañana. *I will do it tomorrow.*

No vendrá. *She _____ come.*

Talking About the Future

The [ ] tense

Use the [ ] to talk about what's
about to happen as well as something [ ].

[ ] + [ ] + [ ]

I'm going to eat the pear.

Susana is going to read a magazine.

Add [ ] to say when you're going to do something.

On Monday, we're going to go to France.

Tomorrow I'm going to swim.

The [ ] tense

Use the [ ]
to say what will happen.

[ ] + [ ]

-ar, -er and -ir verbs	

I will play tennis.

He will take the bus.

They will sell the dog.

Some verbs have a [ ] :

	(to say)	
	(to have...)	
	(to do / make)	
	(to have)	
	(to put)	

	(to want)	
	(to know)	
	(to come)	
	(to go out)	
	(to be able to)	

I will do it tomorrow.

She will not come.

Topic 11 — Grammar

Would, Could and Should

The conditional

The conditional can be used to say ' _____ '. It uses the same stems as the _____ tense.

 irregular future stem / + conditional tense endings

These are the same as the imperfect tense endings for _____ and _____ verbs.

-ar, -er and -ir verbs	
-ía	
-ía	

_____ a Italia.
I would travel to Italy.

Viviríamos aquí.
_____ here.

Use 'poder' (to be able to) in the conditional to say ' _____ '.
Use 'deber' (to have to) to say ' _____ '.

¿Podría ayudarme?
_____ help me?

_____ hacer mis deberes.
I should do my homework.

Combine the conditional with other tenses to make more complicated sentences.

Bailaría, pero _____ los pies.
_____, but my feet hurt.

To say ' _____ ', you need the conditional tense of 'haber' (to have...) and _____ .

Habría comprado un libro, pero no tengo dinero.
_____ a book, but I have no money.

'Quisiera' and 'hubiera'

The conditional form of 'querer' (to want) is often replaced by ' _____ ' to mean 'I would like'. It's often used in _____ .

'Quisiera' and 'hubiera' are in the imperfect subjunctive.

_____ una moto.
I would like a motorbike.

Quisiera reservar una mesa para esta noche.
_____ to reserve a table for tonight.

The conditional of 'haber' (to have...) can also be replaced by ' _____ ' to mean ' _____ '.

Hubiera venido antes.
_____ come earlier.

Topic 11 — Grammar

Would, Could and Should

The

The [   ] can be used to
say 'would'. It uses the [   ]
[   ] as the [   ] future tense.

These are the same
as the ....
....
for -er and -ir verbs.

-ar, -er and -ir verbs

I would travel to Italy.

We would live here.

Use ' [   ] ' (to be able to) in the [   ] to say ' [   ] '.
Use ' [   ] ' (to have to) to say ' [   ] '.

Could you help me?   I should do my homework.

Combine the conditional with [   ]
to make more complicated sentences.

I would dance, but my feet hurt.

To say 'would have...', you need
the [   ] tense of ' [   ] '
(to have...) and a [   ].

I would have bought a book,
but I have no money.

'Quisiera' and 'hubiera'

The [   ] form of ' [   ] ' (to want)
is often replaced by 'quisiera' to mean 'I would like'.
It's often used in [   ].

'Quisiera' and 'hubiera' are in the
....

I would like a motorbike.   I would like to reserve a table for tonight.

The [   ] of 'haber' ([   ])
can also be replaced by 'hubiera'
to mean ' [   ] '.

I would have come earlier.

Reflexive Verbs

Reflexive pronouns

_____ are for actions that you do to yourself. They're used
with _____ , which change depending on who is doing the action.

myself	me	_____	nos
yourself (inf. sing.)		yourselves (inf. pl.)	os
himself / herself / _____ / oneself / yourself (form. sing.)		themselves / each other / yourselves (form. pl.)	

Reflexive verbs are conjugated just like normal verbs.
The reflexive pronoun usually goes _____ the verb.

lavarse (_____)	
te lavas	
se	lavan

_____ la cara cada mañana.
I wash my face every morning.

Se lavan los dientes dos veces al día.
_____ _twice a day._

Here are some common reflexive verbs. The verbs on the left are _____ .

_____ _to go to bed_   _____ _to be called_

despertarse   _____   levantarse

sentirse   _____   _____ _to go away_

_____ _to get dressed_   ponerse   _____

Siempre _____ muy tarde.
You always go to bed very late.

Se despierta a las ocho y media.
_____ _at half past eight._

Reflexives in the _____ tense

Use reflexive verbs in the _____ tense to say what has happened.
Put the _____ in front of the verb as usual.

Me he puesto el sombrero.
_____ _my hat._

Se ha acostado.
_____ .

Topic 11 — Grammar

174

Reflexive Verbs

Reflexive pronouns

Reflexive verbs are for actions that you do ⬚ . They're used
with reflexive pronouns, which change depending on ⬚ the action.

myself		ourselves	
yourself (inf. sing.)		yourselves (inf. pl.)	
himself / herself / itself / oneself / yourself (form. sing.)		themselves / each other / yourselves (form. pl.)	

⬚ are conjugated just like normal verbs.
The ⬚ usually goes in front of the ⬚ .

⬚ (to wash oneself)	

I wash my face every morning.

They brush their teeth twice a day.

Here are some common ⬚ .
The verbs on the ⬚ are radical-changing.

....	to go to bed	....	to be called
....	to wake up	....	to get up
....	to feel	....	to go away
....	to get dressed	....	to put on

You always go to bed very late.   *He wakes up at half past eight.*

Reflexives in the perfect tense

Use reflexive verbs in the perfect tense to say what ⬚ .
Put the reflexive pronoun ⬚ the verb as usual.

I have put on my hat.   *She has gone to bed.*

     ✓ ✓  ✓

Verbs with '-ing' and 'Just Done'

The present continuous

Use the present continuous to describe something that's _____ .

| present tense of '⬚' | + | present participle |

> The present participle (or gerund) is the '_____' part.

Add these endings to the ⬚ to form the present participle.

| ⬚ verbs | -ando | | -er and ⬚ verbs | ⬚ |

Estoy almorzando.
I am _____ .

_____ la mesa.
He is laying the table.

Están escribiendo.
_____ *writing.*

There are some ⬚ present participles that you need to know:

⬚ (to fall)	cayendo	servir (to serve)	
leer (to read)		⬚ (to ask for)	pidiendo
⬚ (⬚)	oyendo	morir (⬚)	
construir (to build)		decir (to say)	
⬚ (to go)		⬚ (to sleep)	durmiendo

The ⬚

Use the _____ to say something was happening in the past. It's similar to the present continuous, but '_____' has to be in the imperfect tense.

Estaba durmiendo cuando sonó el teléfono.
_____ *when the telephone rang.*

Acabar de

To say _____ , use the present tense of 'acabar', followed by 'de' and a verb in the _____ .

Acabo de ducharme.
_____ *taken a shower.*

Verbs with '-ing' and 'Just Done'

The [   ]

Use the [   ] to describe something that's happening right now.

[present tense of ' [   ] '] + [[   ] participle]

The .... (or gerund) is the '-ing' part.

Add these endings to the [   ] to form the [   ].

| -ar verbs | [   ] |

| -er and -ir verbs | [   ] |

I am having lunch.   *He is laying the table.*   *They are writing.*

There are some [   ] that you need to know:

(to fall)			(to serve)	
(to read)			(to ask for)	
(to hear)			(to die)	
(to build)			(to say)	
(to go)			(to sleep)	

The imperfect continuous

Use the imperfect continuous to say something [   ] in the past. It's similar to the present continuous, but 'estar' has to be in the [   ].

She was sleeping when the telephone rang.

VET

[   ]

To say what's just happened, use the present tense of ' [   ] ', followed by ' [   ] ' and a verb in the [   ].

I have just taken a shower.

Topic 11 — Grammar

Mixed Practice Quizzes

If you've spent as much time studying the future as I have, you won't be surprised by what's next: some lovely quizzes to see what you remember from p.169-176.

Quiz 1   Date: ...... / ...... / ......

1) True or false? There are two future tenses in Spanish.

2) Which Spanish verb do you use in the conditional to say 'could'?

3) Translate into English: 'Estabas limpiando la cocina.'

4) How do you say 'Cliff wakes up at half past seven' in Spanish?

5) Where does the reflexive pronoun usually go in a sentence?

6) 'We are going to stay in a hotel.' Say this in Spanish.

7) Give the English for: 'Normalmente pedirías un filete.'

8) What is wrong with this sentence? 'Saberemos más pasado mañana.'

9) 'Acabas de borrar todos los archivos.' Say this in English.

10) How do you say 'We are having dinner' in Spanish?

Total:

Quiz 2   Date: ...... / ...... / ......

1) How do you say 'He goes to bed quite early' in Spanish?

2) True or false? The proper future tense endings are the same for all verbs.

3) Give the Spanish for: 'I am reading a new magazine.'

4) What is the English for 'Esta blusa me quedaría mal'?

5) Translate into English: 'They have just gone out.'

6) What are the present participles of these verbs?
   a) nadar   b) ofrecer   c) construir   d) ocurrir

7) Give the English for: 'Estudiarán arquitectura en la universidad.'

8) Translate into Spanish: 'Would you (inf. sing.) buy a new motorbike?'

9) Give two ways to say 'I would have written more' in Spanish.

10) 'Ya nos hemos lavado los dientes.' Say this in English.

Total:

178

Mixed Practice Quizzes

Quiz 3 | Date: ...... / ...... / ......

1) True or false? The conditional uses the same verb stems as the imperfect tense.

2) How do you say 'Sofía got dressed and put on her coat' in Spanish?

3) Give the Spanish for: 'The flowers are dying because it's too hot.'

4) Translate into English: 'Voy a descargar esta canción.'

5) What are the present participles of these verbs?
   a) oír   b) pintar   c) caer   d) producir

6) Give two ways to say 'I would like a coffee' in Spanish.

7) What is the English for 'Estabais hablando del partido'?

8) What is the proper future stem of the verb 'tener'?

9) Translate into Spanish: 'They are going to visit Toledo next year.'

10) 'I feel tired after riding a bike.' Say this in Spanish.

Total:

Quiz 4 | Date: ...... / ...... / ......

1) Give the English for: 'Saldrás de casa para ir de compras.'

2) 'I am swimming in the sea.' Say this in Spanish.

3) What is the Spanish for 'Paula puts on her coat'?

4) Translate into Spanish: 'You (inf. pl.) should buy more apples.'

5) 'Acabo de almorzar en un restaurante.' Say this in English.

6) True or false? 'Levantarse' is a radical-changing verb.

7) Add a time phrase to this sentence, then translate it into Spanish:
   'Uzma is going to start her Italian lesson.'

8) What are the proper future stems of these verbs?
   a) venir   b) hacer   c) poner   d) poder

9) Translate into English: 'Bailaríamos en la fiesta.'

10) Give the Spanish for: 'My uncle was sleeping when we arrived.'

Total:

Topic 11 — Grammar

Negative Forms

Making sentences negative

To make a sentence negative in any tense, put '   ' in front of the   .

Soy profesor. *I'm a* _____. ⟶ _____ profesor. *I'm not a* _____.

_____ el libro.
You're not going to read _____.

_____ al parque.
I didn't go to _____.

'   ' means both 'no' and 'not' in Spanish. To
answer a question, you may need to say '   ' twice.

_____ sopa, gracias.   *No, I don't want* _____, *thanks.*

More negative constructions

Spanish	English	Example
	no longer *(not anymore)*	_____ voy a Madrid. — *I no longer go to Madrid.*
no ... nadie	_____ *(not* _____ *)*	No hay nadie aquí. — *There is* _____ .
_____ / no ... jamás	*never* *(not ever)*	Julia _____ al cine. — *Julia never goes to the cinema.*
no ... nada	_____ *(not* _____ *)*	No hay nada. — *There is* _____ .
no ... ni ... ni	_____ ... _____	No van ni a Bath ni a York. — *They go to* _____ Bath _____ York.
_____ / _____	*not a single* *— before noun* *(none / not one)*	_____ hay _____ plátano. — *There isn't a single banana.*
_____ ... _____	*not a single one* *— to replace noun* *(none / not one)*	Chen _____ tiene _____ . — *Chen doesn't have a single one.*

Topic 11 — Grammar

Negative Forms

Making sentences negative

To make a sentence negative in any _____ , put _____ the verb.

I'm a teacher. ➡️ I'm not a teacher.

You're not going to read the book.   I didn't go to the park.

'No' means both ' ___ ' and ' ___ ' in Spanish. To _____ , you may need to say ' ___ ' twice.

No, I don't want soup, thanks.

More negative constructions

Spanish	English	Example
	no longer (not anymore)	I no longer go to Madrid.
	nobody (not anybody)	There is nobody here.
	never (not ever)	Julia never goes to the cinema.
	nothing (not anything)	There is nothing.
	neither ... nor	They go to neither Bath nor York.
	not a single — before noun (none / not one)	There isn't a single banana.
	not a single one — to replace noun (none / not one)	Chen doesn't have a single one.

The Passive and Impersonal Verbs

The passive voice

In an active sentence, the subject [____] something.
In the passive voice, something is [____] the subject.

Active voice: Lavé .... [____]
.... the cup.

Passive voice: .... fue lavada.
The cup ....

The passive is formed using '[____]' (to be) and
a past [____]. The past [____] has
to agree with the [____] you're talking about.

.... fueron limpiadas.
The tables ....

To add someone or something doing the action,
add '[____]' (by) and who / what does it.

El libro será leído .... Jordi.   The book .... by Jordi.

Impersonal verbs

You can turn [____] Spanish [____] into an impersonal verb (e.g. 'one does')
by using the [____] pronoun 'se' and the [____] person forms of the verb.

¿Se habla ....?
Does .... French here?

⟵ This can also be translated
as 'Is French [____] here?'

Use the 'he/she/it' form
for [____] subjects...

El arroz .... durante quince minutos.
The rice is cooked ....

...and the 'they' form
for [____] subjects.

Las puertas .... a las nueve.
The doors are opened ....

'Hay que' and 'parece que' are common impersonal verbs.

Hay que hacer ....
Homework ....

Parece que todo ....
.... everything has changed.

[____] verbs are always used in an impersonal way.

Llueve.
....

Está nevando.
....

Truena.
....

⟸ 'Tronar' (to ....) is a
.... verb.

The Passive and Impersonal Verbs

The passive voice

In an active sentence, the subject _____ .
In the passive voice, _____ the subject.

Active voice: | Lavé la taza.

Passive voice: | La taza fue lavada.

The passive is formed using ' ' ( ) and
a _____ . The _____
has to _____ with the object you're talking about.

Las mesas fueron limpiadas.

To add someone or something _____ ,
add 'por' ( ) and who / what does it.

El libro será leído por Jordi.

Impersonal verbs

You can turn _____ Spanish _____ into an impersonal verb (e.g. 'one does')
by using the _____ pronoun ' ' and the _____ forms of the verb.

Does one speak French here? ⟵ This can also be translated as
' _____ '

Use the ' _____ '
form for singular subjects...

The rice is cooked for fifteen minutes.

...and the ' _____ '
form for plural subjects.

The doors are opened at nine o'clock.

' _____ ' and ' _____ ' are common impersonal verbs.

Homework has to be done.

It seems that everything has changed.

_____ verbs are always used in an _____ way.

It rains. | It's snowing. | It thunders.

' .... ' (to thunder) is a
.... verb.

 ✓ ✓ ✓

The Subjunctive

Forming the present subjunctive

For '-ar' verbs, add the [____] tense '-[__]' endings to the stem of the [____] tense 'I' form. For '-er' and '-ir' verbs, add the '-[__]' endings.

hablar — 'I' form: hablo	
hable	hablemos
	hablen

comer — 'I' form: como	
	comamos
comas	

vivir — 'I' form: vivo	
	viváis
viva	

Es importante que ....
.... *you listen.*

No pienso que .... carne.
I .... *he eats* ....

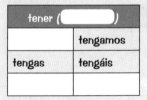

Irregular verbs in the present subjunctive

Some verbs are irregular in the 'I' form of the [____] tense,
so the subjunctive has to [____].

tener ([____])	
	tengamos
tengas	tengáis

[____] (to be able to)	
pueda	
	puedan

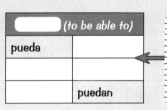

The '...........' and
'...........'
forms of
radical-changing
verbs have
.... stems.

Some verbs are [____] in the subjunctive:

[____] (to be)	sea				seáis	
[____] (to be)		esté	estemos			
ir ([____])		vayas		vayamos		vayan
dar ([____])		des			deis	
[____] (to know)	sepa			sepamos		sepan

 ☑   ☑ 🙂 ☑

184

The Subjunctive

Forming the present subjunctive

For '-ar' verbs, add the [＿＿＿＿＿＿] endings to the stem of the
[＿＿＿＿] 'I' form. For '-[＿＿]' and '-[＿＿]' verbs, add the '-[＿＿]' endings.

hablar — 'I' form: [＿＿]		comer — 'I' form: [＿＿]		vivir — 'I' form: [＿＿]	

It's important that you listen.

I don't think he eats meat.

Irregular verbs in the present subjunctive

Some verbs are irregular in the [＿＿＿＿] of the [＿＿＿＿] tense,
so the subjunctive has to [＿＿＿＿＿].

[＿＿＿＿] (to have)	

[＿＿＿＿] (to be able to)	

The '＿＿＿＿' and
'＿＿＿＿＿'
forms of
＿＿＿＿＿
verbs have
regular stems.

Some verbs are [＿＿＿＿＿＿] in the subjunctive:

[＿＿] (to be)	sea					
[＿＿] (to be)	esté					
[＿＿] (to go)						
[＿＿] (to give)						
[＿＿] (to know)						

Topic 11 — Grammar

The Subjunctive

Use the present subjunctive...

1 ...to get [____] to do something.

> Quiero que ....
> *I want you to wash the dishes.*

2 ...to express a wish or a [____].

> Espero que haya ....
> .... *there are strawberries.*

3 ...after expressing an emotion or [____].

> .... estudiéis.
> *It's important that* ....

4 ...to say that something is [____] to happen.

> No creo que vaya a ....
> .... *she's going to visit us.*

5 ...when there's a requirement.

> .... a alguien que sepa cocinar.
> *I need someone who* ....

6 ...after 'antes de que' ([____]), 'cuando' ([____]) and 'aunque' ([____]) to talk about the future.

> Saldremos cuando lleguen.
> *We'll go out* ....

7 ...after '[____]' (so that) to express [____].

> Salen .... comprar leche.
> *They're going out so that he can buy milk.*

The imperfect subjunctive

The imperfect subjunctive is like the '[____]' in 'if I were you'.

> Si lo describiera, no me creerías.
> *If I* .... *it, you* .... *believe me.*

This is like '**If I** [____] **to** [____] it...'

hablar		comer		vivir	
hablara	habláramos	comiera	comiéramos	viviera	viviéramos
hablaras	hablarais	comieras	comierais	vivieras	vivierais
hablara	hablaran	comiera	comieran	viviera	vivieran

> Era vital que nos escondiéramos.
> *It was* .... *that we* ....

> Dudo que cantaras mal.
> .... *that you* .... *badly.*

 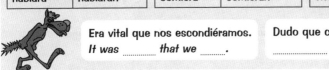

Second Go:
..... / ..... / .....

The Subjunctive

Use the present subjunctive...

1 ...to get _____ to do something.

> I want you to wash the dishes.

2 ...to express a _____ or a _____.

> I hope that there are strawberries.

3 ...after expressing an _____ or _____.

> It's important that you study.

4 ...to say that something is _____.

> I don't believe she's going to visit us.

5 ...when there's a _____.

> I need someone who knows how to cook.

6 ...after ' _____ ' (before),
' _____ ' (when) and ' _____ ' (even if)
to talk about _____.

> We'll go out when they arrive.

7 ...after ' _____ ' (so that)
to express _____.

> They're going out so that he can buy milk.

The imperfect subjunctive

The imperfect subjunctive is like the ' _____ ' in 'if I _____ you'.

> Si lo describiera, no me creerías.

⟵ This is like
'If I _____
_____ ...'

hablara	habláramos		comiera	comiéramos		viviera	viviéramos
hablaras	hablarais		comieras	comierais		vivieras	vivierais
hablara	hablaran		comiera	comieran		viviera	vivieran

Era vital que nos escondiéramos. | Dudo que cantaras mal.

 ✓ ✓ ✓

Giving Orders

Informal commands

To form a singular informal command, take the
' ' off the 'tú' part of the [   ] tense verb.

.... ¡Escucha!
Write! ....

[   ] go at the end of a command, and you need
to add an [   ] to show where the stress is.

¡Cómelo! ....

For plural informal commands, change
the final ' ' of the infinitive to a ' '.

.... ¡Salid!
Read! ....

There are some common [   ] informal singular commands:

[ ] (to say)	[ ] (Say!)	[ ] (to go out)	¡Sal! (Go out!)
[ ] (to do / make)	[ ] (Do! / Make!)	[ ] (to be)	[ ] (Be!)
ir ( )	¡Ve! ( )	tener ( )	¡Ten! ( )
poner ( )	¡Pon! ( )	[ ] (to come)	[ ] (Come!)

Formal commands

For singular formal commands, use the '[   ]'
form of the present [   ]. Use the
'[   ]' form for plural formal commands.

¡Hable! ¡Entren!
....

Some common formal commands are [   ]:

dar ( )	¡Dé! ( )	saber ( )	¡Sepa! ( )
[ ] (to have...)	¡Haya! ( )	[ ] (to be)	[ ] (Be!)
[ ] (to go)	[ ] (Go!)		

Making commands negative

To tell someone not to do something,
always use the [   ].

¡No escuches! ¡No mientas!
Don't _____! *Don't _____!*

Any pronouns have to go [   ]
the verb in negative commands.

¡No _____! ¡No _____!
Don't touch it! *Don't eat them!*

Topic 11 — Grammar

Second Go: ..... / ..... /	# Giving Orders

Informal commands

To form a singular informal command, take the ' ' off the _____ of the _____ verb. *Write!*   *Listen!*

_____ go at the _____ of a command, and you need to _____ an _____ to show where the _____ is.   *Eat it!*

For plural informal commands, change the _____ of the _____ to a ' '. *Read!*   *Go out!*

There are some common _____ informal singular commands:

	(to say)		(Say!)		(to go out)		(Go out!)
	(to do / make)		(Do! / Make!)		(to be)		(Be!)
	(to go)		(Go!)		(to have)		(Have!)
	(to put)		(Put!)		(to come)		(Come!)

Formal commands

For singular formal commands, use the ' _____ ' form of the _____ . Use the ' _____ ' form for plural formal commands.   *Speak!*   *Enter!*

Some common formal commands are _____ :

	(to give)		(Give!)		(to know)		(Know!)
	(to have...)		(Have!)		(to be)		(Be!)
	(to go)		(Go!)				

Making commands negative

To tell someone not to do something, _____ use the _____ . *Don't listen!*   *Don't lie!*

Any pronouns have to go _____ the _____ in negative commands.   *Don't touch it!*   *Don't eat them!*

 ☑ ☑ ☑

Mixed Practice Quizzes

Well, this is it — the last set of quizzes. Before you say 'adiós', see what you can remember from p.179-188. Don't forget to add up your scores at the end.

Quiz 1 | Date: ...... / ...... / ......

1) What do each of these commands mean in English?
   a) ¡Sal!   b) ¡Canta!   c) ¡Bebe!   d) ¡Haz!

2) Translate into Spanish: 'He no longer studies geography.'

3) Explain how to form the present subjunctive in Spanish.

4) What is the difference between the active voice and the passive voice?

5) True or false? The present subjunctive is used to express wishes or desires.

6) Your friend says 'No, no tengo un estuche.' What does this mean?

7) Which of these verbs is in the imperfect subjunctive?:
   • enviarán   • adjuntara   • huelas

8) Say this singular informal command in Spanish: 'Don't annoy your brother!'

9) Give the Spanish for: 'It's important that I go to the concert.'

10) How do you make a Spanish verb impersonal?

Total:

Quiz 2 | Date: ...... / ...... / ......

1) Correct the mistake in this sentence: 'Las manzanas serán cocinado.'

2) Give the English for: 'Era esencial que escribiera la carta yo mismo.'

3) 'They didn't buy the horse.' How would you say this in Spanish?

4) True or false? Formal commands in Spanish use the present tense.

5) Conjugate the verb 'ser' in the present subjunctive.

6) Translate into English: 'El edificio fue construido en el siglo veinte.'

7) Translate this singular informal command into Spanish, replacing the underlined noun with a pronoun: 'Leave <u>the oranges</u> in the kitchen!'

8) Give the English for: 'Sonal has never been to the Canary Islands.'

9) 'Te llamaré cuando termine la película.' Why is the subjunctive used here?

10) Translate into English: 'No creo que mis padres estén equivocados.'

Total:

Topic 11 — Grammar

Mixed Practice Quizzes

Quiz 3   Date: ...... / ...... / ......

1) How would you say 'You (inf. sing.) won't come to the party' in Spanish?
2) 'Gorka quiere que le ayudemos con el repaso.' What does this mean?
3) Translate into English: 'Parece que no hicieron nada.'
4) Give the Spanish for this formal plural command: 'Give me the laptop!'
5) Which forms of radical-changing verbs have
   regular stems in the present subjunctive?
6) 'Cuando estaba en España, no fui ni a Madrid ni a Barcelona.'
   Translate this sentence into English.
7) Give the English for: 'Espero que los niños se comportaran bien.'
8) 'The houses were sold last year.' Say this impersonal phrase in Spanish.
9) Translate into Spanish: 'She opens the door so that the cat goes out.'
10) How do you form a plural informal command in Spanish?

Total:

Quiz 4   Date: ...... / ...... / ......

1) Translate into English: 'Dudáis que su amigo esté contento.'
2) Give the English for: 'El horario es organizado por la jefa.'
3) Which of these verbs have an irregular form in formal commands?
   • escribir   • hablar   • saber   • ir   • poner
4) Change this sentence so that it means 'The shop doesn't sell a single one.':
   'La tienda no vende ningún videojuego.'
5) Translate into Spanish: 'It's worrying that there is so much poverty.'
6) Make this sentence impersonal: 'La Navidad no es celebrada en su país.'
7) True or false? Pronouns in negative commands go before the verb.
8) Give the Spanish for: 'I'm looking for someone who has work experience.'
9) How would you say 'nobody' in Spanish?
10) 'No pensaba que hablaran italiano.' What does this mean in English?

Total:

SPANR41